# Further Education and the Twelve Dancing Princesses

*This book is dedicated to the memory of Ian R.J. Petrie; committed teacher, dance enthusiast, and skilled teller of fairy tales to his adored grandchildren Lyra, Will and Keir.*

'There is not a lot of dancing in FE these days. Neoliberal practices
bite deep into the experience of teachers and students creating much

ur
do
str
st
bo

Ste

f
l

t

L

'M

fu
tc

'T
a

c

in

s'

nt
e

ng
g

et

ts

sm,

and explores the notion of democratic professionalism and how those
working in the sector might reconstruct their profession. It is a rallying cry
for collective action and public protest by those who work in the sector
and are committed to an active and democratized profession. This is a
must-read for students of education, trainee teachers, experienced teachers,
teacher educators, managers and principals.'

**David Powell, Director, The Education and Training Consortium
and HUDCETT**

'How refreshing to read such a provocative, thoughtful and highly original book from FE professionals who value and champion their work – and FE – amidst increasing pressures and restrictions. The twelve chapters, each written by a dancing princess, provide principled, passionate discourse and authentic protest – mature dissent – from "angry and defiant to hopeful and heartening". I hope this book opens a new level of debate, understanding, synergy, practice and thought leadership between FE staff and FE leaders (at every level). It highlights the need to challenge the prevailing political and neoliberal paradigms which restrict our educational ideals and possibilities. I hope many many people in FE, and elsewhere read, engage and dance.'

**Dr Lynne Sedgmore CBE, Executive Director, 157 Group of FE Colleges**

# Further Education and the Twelve Dancing Princesses

Edited by Maire Daley, Kevin Orr and Joel Petrie

A Trentham Book
Institute of Education Press

First published in 2015 by the Institute of Education Press, UCL Institute of Education, University College London, 20 Bedford Way, London WC1H 0AL

ioepress.co.uk

British Library Cataloguing in Publication Data:
A catalogue record for this publication is available from the British Library

ISBNs
978-1-85856-640-5 (paperback)
978-1-85856-662-7 (PDF eBook)
978-1-85856-663-4 (ePub eBook)
978-1-85856-664-1 (Kindle eBook)

Typeset by Quadrant Infotech (India) Pvt Ltd
Printed by CPI Group (UK) Ltd, Croydon, CR0 4YY

Cover and chapter opening images © copyright Wesley Storey, www.wesleystorey.com. Reproduced by permission.

# Contents

# List of abbreviations

| | |
|---|---|
| AE | adult education |
| ALLN | adult literacy, language and numeracy |
| AoC | Association of Colleges |
| APTT | Association of Part-Time Tutors |
| BCF | Building Colleges for the Future |
| BIS | Department for Business, Innovation and Skills |
| CIF | common inspection framework |
| COVE | Centre of Vocational Excellence |
| CPD | continuing professional development |
| CRADLE | Centre for Research and Development in Lifelong Education |
| ESCP | Engage, Support, Challenge, Progress model |
| ESOL | English for Speakers of Other Languages |
| ETAG | Education Technology Action Group |
| ETF | Education and Training Foundation |
| FE | further education |
| FEDA | Further Education Development Agency |
| FELTAG | Further Education Learning Technology Action Group |
| FESC | Further Education Staff College |
| FEU | Further Education Unit |
| GLHs | guided learning hours |
| HE | higher education |
| IfL | Institute for Learning |
| ITE | initial teacher education |
| LSC | Learning and Skills Council |
| LSDA | Learning and Skills Development Agency |
| LSIS | Learning and Skills Improvement Service |
| LSN | Learning and Skills Network |
| LSRN | Learning and Skills Research Network |
| NATECLA | National Association for Teachers of English and Community Language to Adults |
| NATFHE | National Association of Teachers in Further and Higher Education |
| NEET | not in education, employment or training |

| | |
|---|---|
| NIACE | National Institute for Adult and Continuing Education |
| NQT | Newly Qualified Teacher |
| NRDC | National Research and Development Centre for Adult Literacy, Numeracy and Language |
| NVC | non-violent communication |
| OFSTED | Office for Standards in Education, Children's Services and Skills |
| OTL | observation of teaching and learning |
| QA | quality assurance |
| QIA | Quality Improvement Agency |
| SSRs | staff–student ratios |
| TFP | Total Factor Productivity |
| UCU | University and College Union |
| WEA | Workers' Educational Association |

# About the contributors

## Gemma Breed

Gemma teaches dance in post-compulsory education and is currently the programme leader of a Higher National Certificate in Dance at the City of Liverpool College. She has previously worked in the primary, secondary and community dance sectors. She performs as part of the collective 'us geese are swans'.

## Frank Coffield

Frank retired in 2007 after 42 years in education as a teacher, culminating in Professorships of Education at the universities of Durham and the Institute of Education, University of London (as it then was). He has written books on juvenile gangs, the so-called 'cycle of deprivation', drugs and young people, vandalism and graffiti, the impact of policy on the learning and skills sector, learning styles and public-sector reform. Since his retirement he has written: *Just Suppose Teaching and Learning Became the First Priority…* (LSN, 2008); *All You Ever Wanted to Know About Teaching and Learning But Were Too Cool to Ask* (LSN, 2009); *Yes, But What Has Semmelweis Got to Do with My Professional Development as a Tutor?* (LSN, 2010); *From Exam Factories to Communities of Discovery: The democratic route* (IOE, 2012) with Bill Williamson; and *Beyond Bulimic Learning: Improving teaching in further education* (IOE, 2014) with Cristina Costa, Walter Müller and John Webber.

## Maire Daley

Maire taught in FE for more than 30 years. Before retiring in September 2014 she was the programme leader and centre manager for teacher education and initial teacher training in the City of Liverpool College. Throughout her teaching career Maire has been an active trade unionist and was a member of the National Executive Committee (NEC) in NATFHE and UCU. In UCU she was elected to the chair of the Education Committee, and was a member of the Women's, LGBT and International Committees. As a feminist and a socialist her research interests can be summarized as focusing on education for liberation and the democratization of education.

# Beatrix E. Groves

Bea has taught in adult and further education for over 30 years. She is former President of the Institute for Learning (IfL), one-time General Secretary of the Association of Part-Time Tutors (APTT), and is very active in initial teacher training. She is fascinated by the philosophy of Ludwig Wittgenstein, the politics of Herbert Marcuse and the psychology of Daniel Kahneman. She lives in the north-east of England. She still tutors for the Workers' Educational Association (WEA).

# Rania Hafez

Rania is a British-Lebanese writer and academic. Her career in teaching started as a part-time lecturer and trainee teacher at Lewisham College, moving on through the FE ranks to become Head of the Department of Health and Care at Southwark College. In 2004 Rania joined HE as an FE stowaway, eventually heading teacher education for FE as Director of Post Compulsory Education at the University of East London. She is currently Senior Lecturer in Education at the University of Greenwich and visiting research fellow at the universities of Derby and New Buckinghamshire. Rania has held several key national roles in education; she was Non-Executive Director of the Institute for Learning (IfL) until its closure in October 2014, chair of the Standing Committee for the Education and Training of Teachers (SCETT) (2012/13), and has been co-chair of the Learning and Skills Research Network (LSRN) for London and the South East for the past four years. In 2009 Rania founded the professional network Muslim Women in Education.

# Yvonne Hillier

Yvonne is Professor of Education, University of Brighton. She is a founder member of the national Learning and Skills Research Network (LSRN). She has researched teaching and learning in post-compulsory education including basic skills practice, national vocational qualifications, initial teacher training, and work-based learning. She is author of *Reflective Teaching and Adult and Further Education*, 3rd edition (Continuum, 2012), *All You Ever Wanted to Know About FE Policy* (Continuum, 2006), *Changing Faces of Adult Literacy, Language and Numeracy: A critical history* (with Mary Hamilton) (Trentham, 2006) and *Adult Literacy, Numeracy and Language: Policy, practice and research* (edited with Mary Hamilton and Lyn Tett)

(Open University Press – McGraw Hill, 2006). A new *Reflective Teaching in Further, Adult and Vocational Education* (with Professor Maggie Gregson) will be published in 2015 by Bloomsbury. Her current research involves working with community partners and parent researchers examining the effects of educational regeneration.

## Julie Hughes

Julie is Head of Department for Post-Compulsory Education at the University of Wolverhampton with responsibility for Initial Teacher Education and CPD provision for colleagues in the Lifelong Learning Sector. Julie's practice and research explores the role of Web 2.0 technologies such as e-portfolios and blogs, and their attendant dialogic pedagogies. She is particularly interested in how these hybrid learning and teaching practices might support transitions into the university and/or 'HEness' – and into the workplaces of new teachers. Julie is a Higher Education Academy National Teaching Fellow (2005).

## Rebecca Maxted

Rebecca is Head of Chapeltown Academy, a new sixth form in North Sheffield. She was previously Head of Academic Studies at Tameside College and has worked in FE and HE for 20 years. She has overseen several FE departments, including Teacher Education, A levels and Access, and she spent several years training teachers and lecturing on a degree in education. She has also taught a range of social science and humanities subjects, including sociology, religious studies, theology, philosophy and citizenship, at A level and/or in HE. Her current academic interests include A levels, critical education and education policy, as well as the boundaries between the public and private spheres and how these are affected by dominant notions of professional practice. She studied theology and religious studies at the University of Cambridge and is currently completing a doctorate in policy and pedagogy in FE at the University of Huddersfield.

## Lou Mycroft

Lou was determined at school that she didn't want to be a teacher, but washed up at the Northern College via a circuitous route and has stayed there for 15 years, developing new approaches to social-purpose education. For much of this time, she resisted the label 'academic' before finally embracing it – with the modifier 'practical' – to fly a flag for working-class perspectives on the transformational power of education. Lou has developed the TeachNorthern model of social-purpose education and organizes teacher education and professional development programmes at the Northern College. She retains an interest in the development of reflexive diversity programmes and has contributed to a number of publications and blogs on themes of transformation. Lou is a qualified Thinking Environment coach and consultant.

## Matt O'Leary

Matt is Principal Lecturer and Research Fellow in Post-Compulsory Education in the Centre for Research and Development in Lifelong Education (CRADLE) at the University of Wolverhampton. He has worked as a teacher, teacher educator and educational researcher for over 20 years in England, Mexico and Spain. Matt's research interests are rooted in teacher development, particularly exploring the relationship between education policy and the practice of teachers. He is regarded as one of the first educational researchers in the UK to investigate and critique the practice of graded lesson observations. He is also the author of the highly acclaimed book *Classroom Observation: A guide to the effective observation of teaching and learning* (Routledge, 2014).

## Kevin Orr

Kevin is a Reader in Work and Learning at the University of Huddersfield where he has worked since 2006. Prior to that he spent 16 years as a teacher in FE colleges in and around Manchester, mainly on English as a Second or Other Language (ESOL) and teacher-education courses. His research interests remain focused on FE and vocational education and training. His most recent study is of the advice and guidance provided to young people who go on to take vocational courses. He has been a branch officer for NATFHE and UCU throughout his career.

## Damien Page

Damien began his teaching career in a large inner-city FE college in London as a Lecturer in English Language and Literature. He worked as a teacher and manager in a range of areas beginning with A levels and access to social science and humanities, and ending his time in FE as manager of

Entry to Employment construction provision. He then worked as Learning and Curriculum Manager at Linking London at Birkbeck, University of London, developing one of the largest Lifelong Learning Networks in the country, forging partnerships and progression routes between FE and HE institutions. Following this, Damien became a Senior Lecturer in Post-Compulsory Teacher Training at the University of Greenwich, leading the distance-learning PGCE. He is currently Head of Department of Education and Community Studies at Greenwich and his research interests include management and organizational behaviour in education.

## Joel Petrie

Joel has taught in the post-compulsory sector in the North West for 20 years, initially with disabled students and then as a teacher educator. He has held elected college, regional and national NATFHE and UCU positions for much of his career, most recently on the national UCU Disabled Members Standing Committee. He is currently the Advanced Lecturer for HE in the City of Liverpool College, and is studying for an educational doctorate at Huddersfield University.

## Rob Peutrell

Rob is an ESOL and language support teacher in an FE college in the East Midlands and has worked in English language education for over 25 years. He is an active member of UCU and has a history of involvement in grassroots, community-based campaigns. He was a founder member of the Nottingham and Nottinghamshire Refugee Forum and participated in the Action for ESOL campaign. He is a socialist with libertarian leanings and believes strongly that FE should be shaped by democratic values and practices and a commitment to social justice.

## Doug Rouxel

Doug is currently lecturing in music technology at Staffordshire University, but he previously lectured at South Essex College. Doug was a lead member of the campaign to return trade union recognition to the college. In 2009 UCU was recognized by South Essex College after a gap of 13 years and Doug was elected branch secretary and he also became an FE member of UCU's National Executive Committee (NEC) prior to his move to HE. While on the NEC Doug took a very active role in the campaign against the fees that the Institute for Learning (IfL) was proposing to charge. The discussions and debates that came out of this campaign have informed his approach to change within FE. Doug's other work ranges from gallery-based sound art installations to a book on home brewing.

## Rob Smith

Rob is a Principal Lecturer in Post-Compulsory Education in the School for Education Futures at the University of Wolverhampton and co-founder of the Centre for Research and Development in Lifelong Education (CRADLE). He has taught in secondary, FE and HE settings. Recent research has explored how communities of practice can be developed and used to support Skills for Life practitioners in teaching and mentoring. His writing to date has focused on the use of quasi-market mechanisms to organize and regulate the post-compulsory sector. He is interested in the politics and policy of education and, in particular, in the instrumentalization of the sector and the development of resistant educational identities in response to this. By establishing communities of practice, he writes collaboratively with practitioners to explore how values and culture can be energized to counter the worst excesses of marketization and funding-driven provision.

## Wesley Storey

Wesley is a published photographer with an international portfolio who is based in Liverpool, England. He left FE teaching in 2005 and accidentally became a photographer in 2009. He now specializes in documentary photography and informal portraiture. Recent publications have featured in fROOTS, WOW 24/7, the *Liverpool Echo*, the *Sunday Telegraph*, and *In the Footsteps of Giants*, the official photographic book celebrating the event *Sea Odyssey: Giant Spectacular* in Liverpool in 2014.

## Dan Taubman

Dan retired from his post as Senior National Education Official with NATFHE and UCU at the end of 2013. He had held this post for 19 years. Before that he had worked as a field worker, middle and senior manager in Inner London adult education where he helped pioneer community education and outreach strategies. In his work for NATFHE and then UCU he was responsible for formulating policy across further and adult education, drafting the union's submissions to all FE and adult education consultations, and specialized in issues around funding and governance in FE. Following the dispute between UCU and the Institute for Learning (IfL) in 2011/12 he started exploring the issue of professionalism, publishing a UCU policy on professionalism in 2013. Following his retirement from UCU, he has a visiting associate research post at the UCL Institute of Education, University College London, and is continuing his work on professionalism.

## *Jane Weatherby*

Jane spent more than ten years working in the voluntary and community sector. She has been a Development Worker and Tutor Organizer at the Northern College for Residential and Community Adult Education since 1998. During that time she developed and taught programmes of study for community and trade-union activists, workers and groups, on a variety of themes around creating change, as well as teaching women's studies, media, sociology, and social inequalities to access, to HE students. More recently she has worked as a teacher educator, BA in Education course leader and HE coordinator at the college, on a programme designed for people teaching for a social purpose. Jane studied as a mature student with the Open University, completing an interdisciplinary first degree followed by a Masters in Education. She has contributed to a number of books and blogs on education, and remains passionate about the transformative power of education.

# Acknowledgements

Matt O'Leary would like to thank UCU for giving their permission to use some of the data from a national research project that was commissioned and funded by UCU, of and for its members.

Dan Taubman acknowledges the support and input in presenting his work as a chapter to colleagues in and outside UCU, in particular Paul Cottrell, the then UCU Head of Policy, Professor Ken Spours of the UCL Institute of Education, Joel Petrie and Maire Daley of the City of Liverpool College, Bea Groves the former President of IfL, participants at UCU's seminar on professionalism in 2013, and colleagues contributing to the Compass-NUT Inquiry on Education.

Rob Peutrell would like to thank Tish Taylor of Reflect ESOL for permission to reproduce the flyer on page 144; Zaibun Arab, Marketing Officer at Greenwich Community College, for the photograph on page 146; ESOL teacher Khadijah Amani, for the photograph on page 148; and Paul Mackney, former General Secretary of NATFHE / UCU, for the photograph on page 152. He would also like to thank Anna Wilson and Melanie Cooke, two other dancing princesses involved in Action for ESOL, for reading and commenting on the first draft of his chapter.

Maire Daley, Joel Petrie and Kevin Orr extend their thanks to colleagues and students in the City of Liverpool College and the University of Huddersfield's Education and Training Consortium. We also wish to acknowledge the invaluable guidance and support from publishing staff at Trentham and the UCL Institute of Education, in particular Gillian Klein, Jonathan Dore, Sarah Chatwin and Chandrima Ghosh, who have been a pleasure to work with. Finally, special thanks are due to the twelve former FE dance students whose photographs and reflections on what FE means to them so enrich this book: Phillip David Ashby, Heidi Billingsley, Nicola Rea Davis, Ithalia Forel, James Furlong, Rowena Gander, Kieran Howard, Jennifer Meredith, Nathan Roberts, Pei Tong, Lauren Tucker and Stephenie Wiggins.

*'The less you eat, drink and read books; the less you go to the theatre, the dance hall, the public house … the greater is your alienated life – the greater is the store of your estranged being.'*

(Karl Marx)

# Preface
## Frank Coffield

There is a compelling story of civic courage and political protest that is part of the intellectual heritage of every German citizen, but which is virtually unknown in the United Kingdom. In particular, every German teacher and student knows about *Die Göttingen Sieben*, the seven professors from the University of Göttingen who signed a public protest against the king's annulment of the Constitution of Hanover in 1837.

The story deserves to be told in some detail, which will also explain its relevance to the twelve dancing princesses and the chapters that follow. In June 1837 William IV, King of the United Kingdom and Hanover, died; he was succeeded in the UK by Queen Victoria, and in Hanover by her reactionary uncle the Duke of Cumberland, who became King Ernest Augustus. Victoria could not inherit the throne of Hanover because of the Salic Law which barred females from ruling.

The Duke of Cumberland considered the Duke of Wellington to be a dangerous moderate and had been described by a London newspaper of the time as the perpetrator of every crime except suicide. Within two weeks of inheriting the throne, he declared that he did not feel bound by the constitution, which had been agreed by his predecessor in 1833. Later in the same year of 1837 he repealed the constitution, although he had guaranteed absolute adherence to it on his accession. Seven professors (out of a total of 41) from the University of Göttingen felt themselves bound by the oath they had taken to the former constitution, lodged 'a most humble complaint' with the king and refused to take the oath of allegiance to him.

The brothers Jacob and Wilhelm Grimm were leading members of the Göttingen Seven, who were all tried by the University Court for their 'protest of conscience' and then dismissed from their posts by the king. Three of them, including Jacob Grimm, were given three days to leave the kingdom and were sent into permanent exile from the state of Hanover.

In 1837, the Brothers Grimm were neither political philosophers nor activists, but middle-aged philologists, librarians and Germanists who were best known for their *Children's and Household Tales*, the world's greatest collection of over 200 fairy tales, which includes the story of 'The Twelve Dancing Princesses'. Philip Pullman described these tales as having 'the quality that the great pianist Arthur Schnabel attributed to the sonatas of Mozart: they are too easy for children and too difficult for adults'

(2012: xxi). As linguists who thought that the German language would help to unite the German states, they had also begun to compile the first German dictionary, which at the time of Jacob's death in 1863 had reached only the letter F. They were stirred to political action to defend the three fundamental ideas pursued by German universities: *Lehrfreiheit* (freedom to teach); *Lernfreiheit* (freedom to learn); and *Wissenschaft*, defined by Matthew Arnold as 'scientific knowledge systematically pursued and prized in and for itself' (quoted by Paulin, 1990: 6). They further argued that it was so much in the interest of the state to promote and foster these ideals that the state should itself become 'the guarantor of independent and disinterested scientific endeavour' (Paulin, 1990: 10).

The seven professors must also have been deeply insulted, as moderate and devout Christians, to be dismissed by the king as no better than '*Huren und Tänzerinnen*' – whores and dancing-girls, the two nouns no doubt being used as synonyms. Certainly in the eyes of the king they were far from being princesses. These two retiring archivists and professors of linguistics stepped out of the comfort and protection of their ivory tower and publicly defended academic freedom 'in the face of the crude deployment of power' (Paulin, 1990: 22).

Their dismissal created a public sensation, not so much in Hanover itself as in the rest of Germany and Europe, a sensation which was in large measure the result of their students reproducing thousands of copies of their letter of protest and disseminating them widely. Their liberal colleagues in other German universities drew up subscription lists to help them financially and three years later in 1840, the two brothers were offered posts at the University of Berlin, where they settled. In Germany to this day the Göttingen Seven are celebrated as heroes of civic courage, standing up for their convictions in the cause of freedom at considerable personal risk and financial loss. They are also seen as significant forerunners of the first all-German parliament in Frankfurt-am-Main in 1848 and the notion of a liberal, German republic, free from the arbitrary display of royal power.

What have I learned from this cause célèbre, which is commemorated in Germany in books, films and public monuments? First, the power of solidarity: they acted in concert, because seven professors are not so easily picked off as one might have been; and they received financial support from like-minded colleagues throughout Germany. Second, they issued a *public* protest in the full knowledge that they were risking both financial and personal security. Third, with the active support of their students, they turned their principled stand from a local, personal problem into a national and international issue, just as Rob Peutrell describes in Chapter 11 the campaign to save ESOL. Fourth, they argued that academics have a broad civic responsibility, way beyond the confines of the academy, to uphold freedom in the interests of all. Fifth, they acted as quiet, dignified models of personal courage who stood up against arbitrary royal power and in the process learned what freedom means by struggling to retain it. 'Resistance is fertile', as Maire Daley puts it in her chapter. Finally, a number of contributors to this volume speak of feeling isolated within their institution because so many of their colleagues opt for cynical compliance. It is at such times that we need to remember that we can build on the rich legacy of protest from the past. Indeed, most of the chapters that follow describe cases of successful resistance: 'they are contemporary examples of a long line of work that has stretched over more than a century', as Apple and Beane state when discussing equivalent cases in the USA (1995: 19).

There is a real hunger within the further education (FE) and skills sector for news of colleagues who have struggled and succeeded. The chapters that follow contain inspiring examples of principled dissent, powerful alternatives and innovative models, all of which have had to be fought for, but which are undoubted success-stories that need to be better known throughout the education system. This book will help to assuage that hunger.

There is no need for me to draw out the main themes that run through these chapters because that has already been expertly done by Yvonne Hillier in the Conclusion. Instead, I want to make a comment on the language used by the contributors, which veers within chapters from the angry and defiant to the hopeful and heartening. Some of the terms used, for example, are 'toxic', 'oppression', 'embattled', 'hand-to-mouth environment', 'casualized contracts', 'subversion', 'omnipresent' and 'punitive surveillance', 'heightened accountability', 'inauthenticity', students as 'funding fodder', 'the trickle-down theory of education', 'foyer-ism', 'fabrication', 'fragmented knowledge', 'damaged and stunted lives', 'a culture of fear', 'vilified', 'static social mobility', 'victims', 'crisis', 'boycott', 'unethical behaviour', 'over-assessment', 'resistance', 'disputes', 'industrial action', 'backlash', 'animosity', 'cynicism', 'deprofessionalization', 'redundancies', 'acrimonious', 'impotence', 'concerted attack', 'fellow prisoners', 'frontline', 'incarceration', 'self-flagellation', 'downtrodden, disheartened and disempowered', 'erosion of self-confidence', 'chaotic sector', 'survival', 'fundamental opposition', 'protest' and 'worst excesses of policy'. What an indictment of the policies pursued by all the political parties and the practices of some senior managers. No one reading this list could reasonably claim that the FE and skills sector is healthy and in good spirits. The opposite is true: it is a sick sector which is likely to become even sicker unless there are some fundamental changes to government policy and institutional governance.

That, however, is far from being the whole story. These same chapters, which accurately detail every malaise from which the sector is suffering, also contain powerful, positive metaphors, measures and movements such as: 'the dynamic nucleus of the community', 'education as the practice of freedom', 'effective campaigns', 'strong desire for social justice', 'a curriculum driven by students', 'collaborative action', 'critical education', 'professional expertise', 'bottom-up responsibility for innovation', 'playful exploration', 'a positive, alternative ideology', 'passionate hopefulness', 'transformation', 'active resistance', 'innovation and development', 'a culture of openness and critical analysis', 'empowering professional learning', 'social learning spaces', 'autonomy of the collective', 'use of social media in campaigning', 'a strong collective identity', 'qualified, knowledgeable, committed professionals', preparing students for 'active, democratic citizenship', 'collegiate sharing of good practice', 'principled pragmatism', 'reclaiming and reframing our professionalism', 'trusting relationships', 'tutors as guardians of progressive values', 'agents of change', 'moving from subversion to revolution', 'FE as a fairy godmother', 'principled infidelity', 're-claimed and re-energized identities' and 'deliberative spaces'.

The struggle over the coming years will be to ensure that these positive images, proposals and practices prevail over those that are currently creating such harm. The task is to turn moments of resistance into a mass movement (Horn, 2014). The following chapters are not just full of alternative ideas, strategies and examples of successful resistance which will inspire generations of FE tutors; they are creative and courageous contributions, enlivened by hope, a spirit of generosity, and human values which sum up education at its best. I am proud to make common cause with all the contributors to this volume who today are part of the noble tradition of principled dissent, exemplified all those years ago by the Göttingen Seven.

9 October 2014

# References

Apple, M., and Beane, J. (1995) *Democratic Schools*. Alexandria, VA: Association for Supervision and Curriculum Development.

Horn, B. (2014) 'Moments or a Movement? Teacher resistance to neoliberal education reform'. *Forum*, 56 (2), 277–86.

Paulin, R. (1990) *Goethe, the Brothers Grimm and Academic Freedom: Inaugural lecture*. (9 May) Cambridge: Cambridge University Press.

Pullman, P. (2012) *Grimm Tales for Young and Old*. London: Penguin.

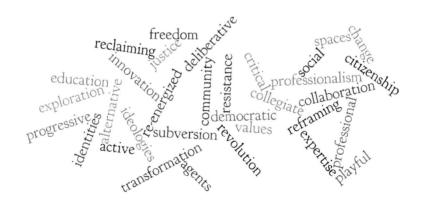

# Introduction:
# How Grimm is FE?
*Joel Petrie*

'*A good dancer is always ahead of the beat. They make the music happen.*'

(Christopher Walken)

## Once upon a time…

This book was conceived in 2012, the 200th anniversary of the publication of the Grimm brothers' *Die Kinder- und Hausmärchen* (Children's and Household Tales), which included the stories of 'Cinderella' and 'The Twelve Dancing Princesses'. The year 2012 also marked the twentieth anniversary of the Further and Higher Education Act which removed colleges from local government control, arguably the most radical structural and political shift in FE in a generation. There has been noteworthy serendipity around this book's genesis, perhaps appropriately, given the word derives from the fairy tale 'The Three Princes of Serendip'.

Ball and Olmedo advocate a courageous refusal of the mundane, a need to delimit ethical spaces 'in relations with others who share the same discomforts. These others might not be available in the staffroom but they may be within everyday social meetings, union meetings or on social media sites' (Ball and Olmedo, 2013: 94). The book's contributors engaged in just such conversations and debates in that increasingly marginal space, the college staff room; at wider academic and trade union conferences; and on web discussion boards. What linked all of these professional dialogues was the mistrust of and distaste for the metaphor of Cinderella to describe FE. What ultimately sparked the project to life was a misdialled telephone call from Professor Frank Coffield (I had arranged with him to give a keynote at my college shortly before). Once Frank had established who I was, or rather who I was not, I told him about our nascent idea for a book that sought to destroy the idea of FE as the Cinderella sector. 'Good,' said Frank, 'I've always despised the parallel; I'll write the preface for you.' We were, metaphorically speaking, invited to the ball.

## The Cinderella sector

The now dominant fairy-tale metaphor for FE as the Cinderella sector, is generally attributed to Kenneth Baker, Minister of Education under Margaret Thatcher, who in 1989 identified a lack of government focus on the sector (Baker, 1989). Thatcher herself had been the Secretary of State for Education and Science from 1970–4, an era of educational initiatives now largely forgotten in the public consciousness except for her fairy-tale villainy as the notorious children's Milk Snatcher. Subsequent education ministers from the Left and the Right have been equally enthusiastic fairy-story tellers. Alan Johnson argued that New Labour had 'buried forever the understandable description of further education as the "Cinderella" of the education world. This debilitating perception should never have been allowed to take root... Cinderella is now dressed and ready to go to the ball. And the coach will not turn into a pumpkin at midnight' (Johnson, 2006).

David Blunkett (quoted in Dolphin and Clifton, 2010: 4) continued the positive spin in 2010 by suggesting that, while the 'sector was once regarded as the Cinderella sector', the perception has changed, 'and we now have a sector that is growing not only in confidence but also in achievement'. Similarly the Skills Minister, John Hayes, identified 'clear signs that something I've always hoped for is starting to happen, FE and skills are no longer the Cinderella they were once described as' (*FE Week*, 7 February 2014). In 2012 the then Secretary of State for Education, Michael Gove, donned his fairy godmother wings to celebrate that 'FE colleges do wonderful work. For too long, they have been Cinderellas, but under this government they are at last going to the ball' (*The Guardian*, 26 August 2013).

There is a significantly earlier governmental use of the Cinderella metaphor to describe vocational and further education. In 1935 Oliver Stanley, the President of the Board of Education, was quoted in the *Glasgow Herald*: 'It has, I believe, been an old complaint among many concerned with the technical side of education that that part of education has been the Cinderella. Well, the Government is determined that even if there was any truth in that in the past, there shall be none in the future' (*Glasgow Herald*, 4 December 1935). It is evident that the Cinderella metaphor has become deeply embedded in the political discourse about FE.

Wider sector grandees, the academy, the press and policy apparatchiks have not been immune to the allure of Cinderella's glittering glass slipper. Some have used the metaphor to imply a sectoral deficit, while others have suggested that FE's prince has come at last. A few illustrative examples are highlighted here. In 2005 Sir Andrew Foster reflected that, while he had found a sector that was delivering crucial economic and social benefits to individuals and communities, it struggled to articulate its value within a wider policy context: it was a 'Cinderella sector' that did itself 'no favours by moaning' (Foster, quoted in Hillier, 2006: 99). Similarly the Executive Director of the 157 Group argued that there 'were always deficit metaphors for FE: middle child, Cinderella, the bit that filled the gap between schools and universities', but celebrated a new 'fabulous metaphor which is colleges as the dynamic nucleus of the community' (Sedgmore, 2011). Gleeson *et al.* (2005) suggest that there is a powerful ideology of uniqueness about FE, rendering it unified only by being different: arguing that it is the, not a, Cinderella service. Randle and Brady (1997) highlight a paucity of research about a Cinderella sector that is all but invisible in the press, while Kerfoot and Whitehead (1998) too employ the fairy-tale metaphor to describe how FE's absence from the public eye enabled successive Conservative administrations to subject it to a market-managed ideology.

Bathmaker and Avis (2005) argue that FE in the 1990s played an increasingly significant role in both the Conservative and New Labour lifelong learning agenda, reflected in the Kennedy Report (1997) which attempted to bring the FE sector out of its Cinderella role, and to establish FE colleges as central to adult lifelong learning policies. A leading light of the Institute for Learning (IfL) raged against the dying of that professional body's mandatory status, claiming that it had helped the Cinderella sector to shine (*Times Educational Supplement*, 19 April 2011), while another press commentator on the fallout of the sector's professionalism debate suggested that the revocation of the Further Education Workforce Regulations illustrated a sectoral shift towards absurdity: from Cinderella to Alice in Wonderland (*FE Week*, 7 June 2013).

The Cinderella story we are now familiar with is a sanitized and Disneyfied version of that published by the Brothers Grimm. Perhaps the most shockingly unfamiliar aspect of the original story relates to impairment. Cinderella's sisters are persuaded in turn by their mother to amputate parts of their feet to fraudulently squeeze into Cinderella's lost slipper and claim the hand of the prince; only when they begin to haemorrhage does he realize his error. Later the sisters are further impaired for their attempt to gain favour; and for their wickedness and falsehood both are blinded by Cinderella's bird familiars. The FE sector itself has been described in terms of sickness and impairment. Coffield (2007) refers to a hole in the heart of FE typified by a government concern to improve the quality of everyone's learning without any interest in learning itself. More recently he has proposed that FE suffers from bulimia academica, typified by stress, nausea, self-disgust, and an inefficient, ineffective testing regime that is purgative and emetic. Lumby and Samier (2010) argue that the concentration of power in senior posts with an associated obsessive control is a bureaupathological trait that can infect administrations.

Elsewhere, Anderson *et al.* (2003) argued that little is consistent in FE except constant change: it is a sector with IADHD (institutional attention deficit and hyperactivity disorder). In relation to changes in funding, Mager (2010) argues that the sector is moving towards a bipolar system of provision for 16 to 18 year olds and adults. Bush and Middlewood (2005) highlight a politically motivated climate spawning constant innovation where pleas for a period of stability fall on deaf ears; and Fullan (1992) suggests that principals are blinded by their own vision. For Ball (2006) there is a structural schizophrenia of values and purposes in which only outputs have value, with beliefs representing an increasingly unimportant and displaced discourse. Senge (2006), describing organizations more widely, famously argued that they learn poorly and have as a result fundamental learning disabilities, which operate despite the clear talents and commitment of employees. Bolden *et al.* (2009: 273) describe the lived experience of the higher education (HE) lecturer as one of 'dislocation, disconnection, disengagement, dissipation, distance and dysfunctionality'; perhaps for FE teachers disablement is equally applicable.

Coffield *et al.* (2014) have highlighted that the atmosphere in the FE sector is increasingly described by lecturers as toxic. Educational metaphors such as Cinderella describing the FE sector contribute to this toxicity:

> Metaphors function both positively and negatively. They have the power to help create meaning and understanding and to improve how we lead. They also have the power to manipulate, to shut down thinking, to deflect creativity, and to harm. Their very ubiquity, their indispensableness, lends metaphors great power.
>
> (Lumby and English, 2010: 3)

According to Lumby and English, metaphors not only describe leadership, they embody the very act of leading. Cinderella functions as a toxic, dead metaphor for the sector, filling the gap where real cognition and analysis of FE might take place. But we need to go further than simply identifying Cinderella as a dead metaphor; we need to kill off the notion completely by promoting the dance of the princesses; and this attempt to change the metaphor is a collective act of sectoral leadership. Or as Neil Gaiman (paraphrasing Chesterton) put it in 2002: fairy tales are important not because they tell us that dragons exist, but because they tell us that dragons can be destroyed.

## The dancing princesses sector

In the original story by the Brothers Grimm, the twelve dancing princesses are locked in their bedroom every evening by their tyrannical father, the king, but they escape through a secret tunnel to dance all night. As a metaphor for teaching in FE this tale is far more celebratory and resonant than Cinderella: it suggests the possibility of subversion, of autonomy in teaching and learning, and a collective rather than individualist notion of professionalism; even within repressive contexts. In the story, the king's suspicions are aroused by the princesses' dancing slippers which are worn through every morning. He commissions a series of princes to spy on the dancers, but all are fooled into drinking a sleeping draft and lose their heads. Ultimately the princesses are betrayed and exposed by an itinerant soldier who pretends to drink the potion, and observes their illicit dancing in a magical glade with the assistance of a cloak of invisibility. The soldier marries one of the princesses as his reward, and the implication is that the twelve princesses' nocturnal freedom is lost, the dance is at an end, and all will be subject to a domesticated compliance through marriage.

The story of the dancing princesses is thus not unproblematic, but we are arguing for a way of thinking about resistance and freedom advocated by Ball and Olmedo in their analysis of Foucault: liberty is 'created in and through acts of resistance and processes of self-definition', while at the same time recognizing 'the possibilities of power, the fragility of freedom and the limits of contingency and domination, while seeking a space within them' (Ball and Olmedo, 2013: 94). It is also possible to speculate on the possibility of further attempts by the princesses to gain liberty and freedom from patriarchy, as Jeanette Winterson did in *Sexing the Cherry* (1990). In her novel, the princesses are introduced to the novel's protagonist later in their lives: they have lived happily ever after, but not with their royal husbands. Three princesses have left their princes, while five murdered their husbands. One has fallen in love with a mermaid and lives with her in a well, while one husband turned out to be a woman. The eleventh kissed her husband and turned him into a frog, before becoming Rapunzel's witch lover. The final, twelfth, princess absconded from her wedding and appears to have escaped from the story altogether to continue the dance:

Their stories ended, the twelve dancing princesses invited me to spend the night as their guest.

'Someone is missing,' I said. 'There are only eleven of you and I have only heard eleven stories. Where is your sister?'

They looked at one another, then the eldest said, 'Our youngest sister is not here … She was, of all of us, the best dancer, the one who made her body into shapes we could not follow. She did it for pleasure, but there was something more for her; she did it because any other life would be a lie. She didn't burn in secret with a passion she could not express; she shone.

(Winterson, 1990: 60)

It is this sense of dance embodying honesty that we wish to celebrate; specifically as an aspect of our shared professionalism in a community of discovery in which anything other than principled dissent would be a lie; and where sector leaders should 'grow by being challenged, and institutions become mature when members at all levels are able to tell truth to power' (Coffield and Williamson, 2011: 50). To borrow for a moment from Hans Christian Andersen, a contemporary fabulist of the Brothers Grimm, it is time for the sector's professionals to point out when FE's emperors and empresses have no clothes. Coffield identifies six potential professional responses by individuals and colleges to destructive, extreme and confrontational educational environments. The first is compliance: a self-preservatory retreat into safe teaching methods and acquiescence with established institutional practices. He typifies the second as strategic or cynical compliance: where professionals covertly bend the rules to protect students, colleagues and the institution from negative change. The third approach is survivalism, where colleges maximize funding by prioritizing targets above all else, and slavishly follow OFSTED's inspection criteria to pursue 'outstanding' status.

Resistance or subversion may follow when policies or practices so offend professionals' 'basic values that they retreat into whatever spaces they can find, from where they can reassert and celebrate their autonomy' (Coffield *et al.*, 2014: 5). The exit response is to leave FE teaching altogether through early retirement, stress-related impairment, changing career, resignation or promotion to management. This strategy might also cover what Coffield calls internal exile – the small minority of teachers who react to relentless pressures by simply going through the motions. The final, and most positive, response is to become powerful, democratic professionals.

Despite the tightening parameters of working in FE, Coffield argues that lecturers 'will become only as powerful and democratic as the culture within which they work allows them to be; or, to put the point more positively, they will become as powerful and democratic as those educators can achieve through constant, collective struggle' (Coffield *et al.*, 2014: 11).

It has been our collective aspiration that this book represents a powerful, democratic, professional response to the sector's ills. Further, we follow the maxim of Deleuze (1988) that the act of writing about FE is to struggle and resist, to write is to become, to write is to draw a map. We hope that others will travel in the spaces that the book begins to explore. Bill Williamson (2013) has suggested that if social change danced to the tunes of our best ideas we would now be living in paradise, but in recent decades the most effective change agents both generally and in education have been ideologists of the free market. We suggest that this ideological transformation can and should be challenged. Ken Robinson has argued for dedicating equal time in the curriculum to dance and maths, and while this might at first glance appear nonsensical, his insistence on the importance of dance and creativity exposes the limits of curriculum and the need for new educational narratives. For Salman Rushdie (1991), an author who is acutely aware of the potentially dangerous power of stories, unreality may be the only weapon with which reality can be smashed, so that it may subsequently be reconstructed. To reclaim what has been lost in FE we may first need to create stories, invisible spaces and an FE sector of the mind.

## The contributing dancing princesses

Jameson and Hillier point out that FE is 'vastly under-researched in comparison with the data potentially available to it', which contributes to it being overlooked and undervalued; and they call for the lack of opportunity and support for 'research, reflection and publication by its practitioners' to be redressed (Jameson and Hillier, 2003: 3). Similarly, Coffield has criticized the lack of research evidence in FE, asking where else you would find a £10 billion industry with no research. Although academic publication is by no means the sole measure of sectoral research, it is notable that the journals with a focus on FE rarely have more than a few authors from the sector: if FE is researched at all it tends to be from within HE.

It could be argued that scholarly activity is less central to the working life of FE lecturers, and that a greater emphasis on high-quality staff development should be in evidence. However, the account of the history of FE development agencies given by Huddleston and Unwin suggests otherwise. In the period since incorporation such bodies have metamorphosed with dizzying regularity according to the whims of successive governments: the Further Education Staff College (FESC) and Further Education Unit (FEU) merged into the Further Education Development Agency (FEDA); this in turn became the Learning and Skills Development Agency (LSDA), which itself evolved into the Quality Improvement Agency (QIA) and the Learning and Skills Network (LSN); followed by the Learning and Skills Improvement Service (LSIS). Like frenetic fairy godmothers, educational ministers of all political persuasions magically transformed FE's professional bodies from pumpkins into ephemeral carriages, with little apparent regard for sectoral continuity or professional developmental stability. In the meantime there was a laudable attempt to establish a democratic professional body which aimed to be run by the members for the members, but which failed even to mention educators in its own name – the Institute for Learning (IfL). The IfL leadership's Pythonesque insistence that the haemorrhaging of sectoral confidence had been merely a flesh wound, once members were expected to fund the body via fees, was ultimately consistent with its longstanding organizational learning difficulties and, like all of these other sector bodies, it has disappeared. The Further Education Guild (which had something of a fairy-tale or medievalist ring to it), which was to take up some of the functions of the IfL, had hardly impinged on the sector's consciousness before transmogrifying into the more totalitarian-sounding Education and Training Foundation (ETF). It is perhaps appropriate that Wolverhampton University's recently established Centre for Research and Development in Lifelong Education enjoys the acronym CRADLE: the sector urgently requires a more mature, consistent and genuinely developmental approach to staff development and research-based practice.

It was thus an explicit intention to foreground writers from FE in this book: all its contributors have a history at the FE chalk face, and many remain as teachers in the sector. Collectively we intend this approach to constitute a model for a coalition of resistance. The authors of the twelve chapters that follow were invited to identify and celebrate the autonomous and collective professional spaces that can still be exploited and expanded in FE; to consider where professionals might still lead the dance. The chapters are ordered to move broadly from issues of pedagogy to professionalism and ultimately to resistance.

Maire Daley's analysis of the professional aspirations of prospective teacher education students is followed by Bea Groves's account of educational empowerment and teacher autonomy via the development of communities of practice. Rebecca Maxted considers the possibility of drawing inspiration from critical pedagogy to maintain transformative professional spaces, while Julie Hughes analyses the impact of technology on learning, considering how frivolity may be an ethical, critical and practical response to contemporary educational discourses. Jane Weatherby and Lou Mycroft engage in a professional dialogue about community, collectivism, sustainability and hope. Matt O'Leary examines the negative impact of the current managerialist use of lesson observation in the sector, arguing for the potential for lecturers to reclaim observation as a valuable tool for empowerment of professional learning; and Rob Smith interrogates how the physical spaces in which teaching and learning are situated have become a commodified fantasy. Dan Taubman redefines professionalism as encompassing educational values rather than market forces via an activist, democratic approach to communities of practice. Damien Page identifies subversion extending into FE leadership by examining managerial resistance and collusion; and Doug Rouxel analyses the dispute over professionalism and the possibility of wresting back autonomy and professional space. Rob Peutrell examines a teacher-activist model of educational and professional practice; and Rania Hafez considers the restoration of professionalism via increased confidence in pedagogy, autonomy and collective teacher development. Finally, Yvonne Hillier concludes the book by drawing together the findings of the chapters, articulating lessons for practitioners and the sector with specific reference to the work of the Learning and Skills Research Network (LSRN).

The dance photographs were choreographed by Gemma Breed and photographed by Wesley Storey: the twelve dancers are former FE students, representing the sector's wonderful diversity, and their reflections on what FE means to them should shame those policy makers who have redefined FE's mission in increasingly narrow economic parameters.

## And they all taught happily ever after?

Fairy stories can be deadly and they can be deadly serious. In their 2012 trial, the feminist punk dissidents Pussy Riot cited the avant-garde writer Vvedensky as a key influence. Vvedensky faced accusations of writing anti-Soviet children's stories, and was arrested and died during Stalin's Great Purge. In Svetlana Gouzenko's memoir of her Soviet childhood (quoted in Coffield *et al.*, 2014), she describes how her class produced a play in which fairy-tale characters including Cinderella were condemned as unfit for Soviet children and exiled, only for the distressed assembled children to cry for their pardon and return. Zipes suggests that power and oppression are the key concerns of folktales – while they may not unequivocally seek a revolution of social relations, they nevertheless have a utopian aspect in the imaginative portrayal of class conflict, and are rooted in the 'desire to overcome oppression and change society' (Zipes, 2006: 8). The utopian dancing of the twelve princesses is a worthy metaphor for FE teaching and a sector that continues, despite the increasingly neoliberal educational climate, to offer second (and third and fourth…) chances and lifelong learning, and to transform lives.

So can FE live happily ever after? If the sector is to be Grimm it should be so on our own terms: as powerful, democratic, dancing professionals. Warner argues that fairy tales can act as fifth columnists; defying existing structures while proposing alternatives. They offer 'magical metamorphoses to the one who opens the door, who passes on what was found there, and to those who hear what the storyteller brings. The faculty of wonder, like curiosity, can make things happen; it is time for wishful thinking to have its due' (Warner, 1994: 418). It is time for the sector of the dancing princesses to have its due, and for FE's cinders to be reignited.

# References

Anderson, G., Barton, S., and Wahlberg, M. (2003) 'Reflections and experiences of further education research in practice'. *Journal of Vocational Education and Training*, 55 (4), 499–516.

Baker, K. (1989) 'Further education: a new strategy'. Speech presented at the Annual Conference of the Association of Colleges of Further and Higher Education, London, February.

Ball, S. (2006) *Education Policy and Social Class: The selected works of Stephen J. Ball*. London: Routledge.

Ball, S., and Olmedo, A. (2013) 'Care of the self, resistance and subjectivity under neoliberal governmentalities'. *Critical Studies in Education*, 54 (1), 85–96.

Bathmaker, A., and Avis, J. (2005) 'Is that tingling feeling enough? Constructions of teaching and learning in further education'. *Educational Review*, 57 (1), 3–20.

Bolden, R., Petrov, G., and Gosling, J. (2009) 'Distributed leadership in Higher Education: Rhetoric and reality'. *Educational Management Administration and Leadership*, 37 (2), 257–77.

Bush, T., and Middlewood, D. (2005) *Leading and Managing People in Education*. London: Sage.

Coffield, F. (2007) *Running Ever Faster Down the Wrong Road: An alternative future for education and skills*. Inaugural Professorial Lecture. London: Institute of Education.

Coffield, F., and Williamson, B. (2011) *From Exam Factories to Communities of Discovery: The democratic route*. London: Institute of Education.

Coffield, F., Costa, C., Müller, W., and Webber, J. (2014) *Beyond Bulimic Learning: Improving teaching in further education*. London: Institute of Education Press.

Deleuze, G. (1988) *Foucault*. Minneapolis: University of Minnesota Press.

Dolphin, T., and Clifton, C. (2010). *Colleges 2020*. London: IPPR.

Fullan, M. (1992) 'Visions that blind'. *Educational Leadership*, 49 (5), 19–22.

Gaiman, N. (2002) *Coraline*. London: Bloomsbury.

Gleeson, D., Davies, J., and Wheeler, E. (2005) 'On the making and taking of professionalism in the further education workplace'. *British Journal of Sociology of Education*, 26 (4), 445–60.

Hillier, Y. (2006) *Everything You Need to Know About FE Policy*. London: Continuum.

Huddleston, P., and Unwin, L. (2008) *Teaching and Learning in Further Education: Diversity and change*. London: Routledge.

Jameson, J., and Hillier, Y. (2003) *Researching Post-Compulsory Education*. London: Continuum.

Johnson, A. (2006) 'Learn to earn'. Speech presented at the Quality Improvement Conference, Birmingham, June.

Kerfoot, D., and Whitehead, S. (1998) '"Boys own" stuff: Masculinity and the management of further education'. *Sociological Review*, 46 (3), 436–57.

Lumby, J., and English, F. (2010) *Leadership as Lunacy: And other metaphors for educational leadership*. London: Sage.

Lumby, J., and Samier, E. (2010) 'Alienation, servility and amorality: Relating Gogol's portrayal of bureaupathology to an accountability era'. *Educational Management Administration and Leadership*, 38 (3), 360–73.

Mager, C. (2010) 'Governance in times of freedom and devolution'. In conference proceedings, *Organisation and governance in post-compulsory education: Where now for the Coalition Government?* London: Institute of Education. Online. www.ioe.ac.uk/Organisation_and_Governance_Notes.pdf (accessed 12 October 2014).

Randle, K., and Brady, N. (1997) 'Managerialism and professionalism in the Cinderella service'. *Journal of Vocational Education and Training*, 49 (1), 21–139.

Rushdie, S. (1991) *Imaginary Homelands: Essays and criticism 1981–1991*. London: Granta.

Sedgmore, L. (2011) *The change in metaphor used by Ministers when discussing FE*. Video. Online. http://tinyurl.com/p4mo9g2 (accessed 14 October 2014).

Senge, P. (2006) *The Fifth Discipline: The art and practice of the learning organisation*. 2nd ed. London: Random House.

Warner, M. (1994) *From the Beast to the Blonde: On fairy tales and their tellers*. London: Chatto & Windus.

Williamson, B. (2013) 'Reclaiming Our Ground: Democracy and discovery for educators'. Keynote speech at the Liverpool Community College Research Day Conference, 26 April.

Winterson, J. (1990) *Sexing the Cherry*. London: Vintage.

Zipes, J. (2006) *Fairy Tales and the Art of Subversion: The classical genre for children and the process of civilization*. 2nd ed. London: Routledge.

'My experience of FE gave me the hunger to reach for a higher level in my career. On a personal level it provided a vital stepping stone in developing my knowledge of my field.'

Jennifer Meredith

# Chapter 1

# Why teach?
# Not afraid to dance
*Maire Daley*

'If I can't dance I don't want to be in your revolution.'

(Attributed to Emma Goldman)

## Twelve dancing princesses and FE

Teaching in FE colleges has much more to do with the active subversion of the Twelve Dancing Princesses than the fatalistic, happenchance approach of Cinderella, and her fantastic notion that someday her prince will come. Like the princesses, teachers recognize that unacceptable limitations are being placed on their practice and they have to make decisions about how to negotiate them. Often, like the princesses, strategies are discovered collectively. Like teachers in the sector, the princesses in the story are practitioners: while they dance they are activists, their actions result in a version of liberation that is constrained by their semi-captivity, but they are engaged in a conscious, active management of their reality. They are not passive, nor do they theorize about liberation – they construct and experience a version of it. This, I think, is the key link between the story and the modern FE teacher.

## Why teach?

For many years I taught on teacher education programmes at a large inner-city general FE college. When we interviewed students interested in going into teaching we asked them: 'Why do you want to become a teacher?' Students discussed all kinds of wonderful things. Many talked with great passion about the love of their subject and their need to make a difference to people's lives: they wanted to pass things on or pay things back, they discussed social justice and the love of working with people and they often spoke of the real enjoyment of learning that they themselves have. So far we haven't had the response: 'I'd like to subordinate real education to economic imperatives.' I suspect that there is nothing new in the ideals of new teachers – thinking back more than 40 years, these were my motives and those of my fresh-faced colleagues starting out in a Teacher Training College in 1972. A student teacher asked me recently: 'If the sector was like it is now when you were starting out would you have become a teacher?' Why we teach and why we remain teaching are tough questions to answer.

In 2013 my college's teachers were invited to participate in drawing up a teaching and learning strategy: they engaged in a reflective process to identify their thoughts and ideas about effective teaching and learning. A great deal of what they said about their experiences was framed within their reasons (dreams and aspirations) for entering teaching in the first place, even though this may have been decades ago, and comparing this with their lot now (157 Group, 2013). There was strong evidence of their seeing the ideal, echoing bell hooks when she argues:

> The academy is not paradise. But learning is a place where paradise can be created. The classroom with all its limitations remains a location of possibility. In that field of possibility we have the opportunity to labour for freedom, to demand of ourselves and our comrades, an openness of mind and heart that allows us to face reality even as we collectively imagine ways to move beyond boundaries, to transgress. This is education as the practice of freedom.
>
> (hooks, 1994: 207)

Another part of the answer links to notions of public service and that draws deeply on the reasons we come into teaching in the first place. Similarly teachers often invest heavily in what Jackson and Burke outline as the potential of lifelong learning to 'develop social capital, social cohesion and voluntary and community involvement, engaging people in common concerns and leading to social inclusion and neighbourhood renewal' (2007: 51).

In a sense the motivations for continuing teaching are refined versions of the reasons for joining, provided by new teachers.

## Teachers are dangerous people

John Hattie (2003) suggests that the greatest source of variance in relation to student achievement is teachers, greater than other key factors such as home, peers, school or principal. One of the earliest exercises we do in teacher education programmes with new teachers is to ask them to reflect on Hattie's ideas and on their own experiences of learning and to consider the role of the teacher. To encourage this reflection we had put up two banners on the walls: 'Teachers are Dangerous People', and, paraphrased from Paulo Freire: 'There is no such thing as a neutral education, education acts as either a process of domestication or liberation.' These banners were intended to provoke our students and, interestingly, over the years they have been more provocative than we envisaged: the banners were taken down many times – by whom, we don't know. They obviously irritated some people, because they would sneak in to the classrooms when we were not about and remove them.

The reason for the choice of these two particular banners goes back to the time I went with a group of teachers and trade unionists to visit Colombia. The purpose of the visit was to investigate the claim that Colombia is the most dangerous place in the world to be a teacher. It was inspirational to meet teachers and trade unionists who persist with their activities despite death threats, displacement, disappearances, failed assassination attempts on themselves and successful ones on their colleagues. I believe that the reasons for targeting teachers are the same reasons that drive people to become teachers.

Coming back from Colombia made me want to be a better, more dangerous teacher in a place where my well-being was not under threat. The greatest piece of learning for me was that a teacher needs to be conscious in the role and remain sufficiently conscious to maintain a continual challenge to the context of learning. It helps in developing the role as a conscious teacher to reflect on Freire's notions that: 'Education makes sense because women and men learn that through learning they can make and remake themselves, because women and men are able to take responsibility for themselves as beings capable of knowing – of knowing that they know and knowing that they don't' (Freire, 2004: 15). I suspect Freire was a magnificent dancer.

## What are new teachers letting themselves in for?

The following outlines some of the constraints on teachers; there are many more. I have chosen these few as the ones that I believe are important for new teachers to reflect on. Also, it is important that new teachers recognize that the way things are is not the way they have always been. Currently there is a trend to undermine the value of experienced teachers. I believe this needs to be challenged through a professional discussion that does not devalue long service (and long memories), but challenges these in the light of evidence and reflection on practice. These are the backdrop to the dance.

## Some constraints
### *Conditions of working*

Every year there are students in teacher education classrooms all over the country: good, new teachers who would be able to make a valuable contribution to education and their subjects. But they will be very lucky to get a full-time permanent teaching post. They are much more likely to be required to sign up with an agency or accept a zero hours contract and so be limited in their potential through detrimental pay rates, working conditions and the casualization of their work. Year after year they will work under the threat of being laid off with little or no notice, be paid a fraction of the wages of colleagues doing the same job, be asked to teach in places that are essentially hostile, that provide very little support and that offer term-time only contracts and hot-desking, and be expected to pick up classes, drop classes, change sites, travel or work in lunchtimes and other times for no pay, as well as engage in staff development at their own expense. Often they are offered work that is identified as being not the full teaching role, and work as assessors, tutorial advisors or within a range of other constructed roles. They are often doing a teacher's job on a support worker's pay. The density of casualized contracts in the sector is growing to upwards of 40 per cent of teachers (Lingfield, 2012).

## *Student access and curriculum choice*
Who our students are in the sector is changing and this has less to do with changing need and more with how fees and funding enable or inhibit access. The notion of entitlement to education is complicated, but it is clear that government priorities have limited access by prioritizing some age groups and some types of learning. Anne O'Grady sums up shifts in the provision in FE, arguing that:

> Further education provision, over the last decade or so, has moved from one where there was a strong focus on vocational, remedial, second chance or part-time learning for adults, either accredited or not, to one which has become a central and key provider of learning that is driven to meet the economic demands of the country.
>
> (O'Grady, 2013: 62)

The government-commissioned Foster Report (2005) set out the importance of links with business, recommending that FE colleges needed to identify how they intend to best deliver what Foster argued was their primary purpose: 'to improve employability and skills in its local area contributing to economic growth and social inclusion' (Foster, 2005: 10). Foster set out a need for an increased focus on employability and outlined five imperatives for the future of FE: purpose, quality, learners, employers and reputation. Critics of Foster argued that his message was confused and that it called for an unacceptable narrowing of the curriculum. As Bryan and Hayes (2007) argued, it allowed for the McDonaldization of FE.

I think it is useful for new teachers to set the views of Foster alongside those of Freire when he discusses the goals of education. Freire suggests:

> Education should raise the awareness of the students so that they become subjects, rather than objects, of the world. This is done by teaching students to think democratically and to continually question and make meaning from (critically view) everything they learn... Knowing is a social process, whose individual dimension however cannot be forgotten or even devalued. The process of knowing, which involves the whole conscious self, feelings, emotions, memory, affects, an epistemologically curious mind, focused on the object, equally involves other thinking subjects, that is, others also capable of knowing and curious.
>
> (Freire, 2005: 92)

Freire requires us to think about individuals within the process of education, whereas the government requires us to provide evidence of meeting economic imperatives. Criticism of the demand-led employability-driven government agenda does not suggest that vocational education cannot be meaningful and beneficial to students. On the contrary, what matters is that for both Foster and Freire the approach to the process of learning and the content of the curriculum are critical factors for a student. There are dangers in shifting complex vocational education and training into narrow competency-based programmes. Writing about curriculum of vocational education and training in Australia, Leesa Wheelahan (2007) argues that 'competency based training in vocational education and training is one mechanism through which the working class is denied access to powerful knowledge represented by the academic disciplines' (2007: 637).

Academic boards have all but disappeared from FE colleges. A professional discussion about the design and choice of courses is increasingly rare, and is more likely to be reduced to the process of checking the inclusion of the course on the list of approved courses. Thus the current direction of the curriculum disempowers both students and teachers as it raises the economic imperatives above all else. Freire suggests:

> The more education becomes empty of dreams to fight for, the more the emptiness left by those dreams becomes filled with technique, until the moment comes when education becomes reduced to that. Then education becomes pure training, it

becomes pure transfer of content, it is almost like the training of animals, it is a mere exercise in adaptation to the world.

(Freire, 2004: 84)

## Workloads

Changes in the calculations of guided learning hours (GLH) and increased staff–student ratios (SSRs) have resulted in larger classes of students being expected to achieve in shorter times. For example: in the days of beasts and fairies when the magical Silver Book had the power to limit a teaching contract to 21 hours of contact time, an A level course was usually taught in 7 hours per week over a 36-week year. So an A level teacher would be required to teach three groups of between 10 and 15 students. Now these courses are taught in 4 or 4.5 hours a week over a 30- or 32-week year with a teaching contract that is likely to include 23 or 24 contact hours per week and an annualized hours contract averaging around 830 hours. A teacher could be responsible for six groups of around 20 students, almost trebling their workload.

There is a lot wrong with the current FE sector and with the education system generally. Compass and NUT (2014), in their Inquiry into a 21st Century Education System, call for radical transformation of the whole of education, based on their view of what is not right with our current education system.

> It is too centralized, competitive, individualized and backward looking. More importantly, successive governments, and in particular the current Coalition Government, have run education in England in such a way that the transformative and social potential of education is not realized. Power has become highly concentrated in the hands of ministers, resulting in constant politically and ideologically imposed change, which demoralizes teachers, confuses students and parents, and marginalizes key stakeholders like the business community.

(Compass and NUT, 2014: 6)

## The dance

Did the Princesses dance well? How did they know?

### Reflection on practice

A good teacher education programme mixes theory and practice to build a discipline of reflecting on practice. It builds in time to theorize, experience and discuss practice. Following my Colombian experience, I developed my own version of reflective practice based on the reflection of the notion of the conscious teacher. This has worked for me and some of the associated ideas are outlined further in this chapter's conclusion. Freire suggests:

> It is by exposing what we do to the light of the knowledge that science and philosophy offer that we correct and perfect ourselves. It is this that I call 'thinking the practice', and it is by thinking the practice that I learn to think and to practice better.
>
> (Freire, 2005: 140)

Professional discussion between a teacher and anyone else should be democratic; Coffield outlines this in what he defines as the 'powerful, democratic professional' (2014: 8). I recommend that all teachers construct their own (or teaching team's) notion of what it means to be a reflective practitioner and that this be done within a context of collaboration rather than force. Reflection on practice is, I suggest, activism.

## Collective action

Alongside confident reflective practitioners, there is a key role to be played by trade unions. The ability to discuss collectively – in branches, regions and nationally – is essential to understanding the context of teaching in the sector. I believe it is high time that a call is made to establish stronger collaboration between school-teachers' unions and the University and College Union (UCU) – maybe even a merger. We have to draw together the experiences across all sectors of education if we are to maximize our power in the dance.

We can look to UCU, as a campaigning union, for many examples of effective campaigns. I'd like to draw on two examples, because they could be seen as unsuccessful.

Example 1

UCU's *Manifesto for Post-School Education* (2010) set out a vision for the future of education founded on the fundamental belief in the intrinsic value and power of education to be a force for good. The manifesto was constructed in a context of cuts across public services, with education bearing the brunt. It was launched at a parliamentary lobby and formed the keystone of the union's campaign to encourage parliamentary candidates to clearly state their position on education so the electorate could make an informed choice at the general election. The Manifesto made a strong statement about the value and the place of post-school education and led to national and local campaigns, involving union members in meetings with candidates. Notably, many Liberal Democrat parliamentary candidates (including their leader) signed pledges to remove student fees.

EXAMPLE 2

The Save Adult Further Education (SAFE) campaign in Liverpool, 2006 (UCU, n.d.) arose in response to the local FE college's proposal to cut a longstanding and highly successful Second Chance to Learn programme. At the same time a national campaign, the Campaigning Alliance for Lifelong Learning (CALL), was also being set up to highlight similar concerns across the country. Both campaigns were joint actions between teachers and students and were supported by UCU. In Liverpool a highly visible campaign was launched to try to protect the Second Chance to Learn courses in the college. Actions included lobbying parliament, writing letters to MPs and setting up a website highlighting the experiences of past students. A charter was collectively devised and students, past and present, teachers, local politicians and members of the local community signed up to it. A film made by students (see SAFE, n.d.) was launched at the TUC – held in Liverpool that year – and questions were asked in the House by local MPs. The campaign was picked up by local press, TV and radio and the national press. It was a wonderfully engaging campaign – a brilliant dance. Second Chance to Learn is no longer a unique stand-alone programme in the college; however, parts of it have been integrated with a more general offer.

Both these initiatives essentially failed to achieve their goals, but I've included them here as truly effective collective actions because they required a huge amount of learning by the activists. I believe every teacher involved in these campaigns became a better teacher because of it. The process as well as the outcome needs to be valued. Resistance is fertile.

## A manifesto for teachers

I recommend that all teachers new and old develop their own ways of articulating the parameters (the music and the form) of their own dance. It should list, set out and put actions against the values and beliefs that influence their approach to teaching their subject – or even better, do it as a team. It should be constantly challenged and periodically revised. Below is the last incarnation of the teacher education dance drawn up by the team with which I worked:

> The ethos and values of the programme team in relation to teaching and learning are ones that will promote cultures of learning by ensuring that by the end of the programme the student teacher will be offered opportunities to:

- see their role to be broad with a sense that learning will equip students for life
- take responsibility to be up-to-date in their subject specialism
- develop their own approach to teaching that identifies the best ways of teaching to enable students to develop a critical engagement with the subject
- take account of what their students bring with them to learning, by recognizing the personal and cultural experiences of their students
- devise ways to provide support for students to develop independence in learning
- use assessment to advance learning as well as a measure of achievement
- provide active engagement in learning to enable students to become an agent in their own learning
- contextualize learning and link to students' broad life experiences so they draw on learning within the classroom and beyond it
- continue their own learning based on feedback and reflection on their own practice and encourage reflection in their students
- identify that teaching and learning is at the heart of their professional practice
- remember their passion.

This is not a recipe, it is a dance, so it can be interpreted and improvised on by any of the dancers.

## Why dare to dance?

In Colombia I was asked to contribute to the closing address at the Human Rights Forum, on 26 April 2003 in Bogotá, on behalf of the delegation. We had heard about individual teachers and students being assassinated (students shot in their classrooms and teachers shot in front of their students), of disappearances, displacements and forced exiles (Justice for Columbia, n.d.). The day before, as if to encapsulate all this, we learned that Luz Elena Zapata, a teacher, was taken off the school bus and shot dead in front of her students. Struggling towards an understanding of this act, I noted that the delegation had asked:

> Why teachers, why students? We reflected on our own roles and experiences as teachers. We considered our own motives and the reasons why we have a passion for teaching, and concluded: we

love to see students grow, to open up to new ideas and be critical of ways of thinking. For students to know their place in history, to examine their place in the world and to really think about their place in the future – this is the real purpose of education.

So this is why we teach and why we are not afraid to dance. The challenge for teachers, experienced as well as new, is to work to construct safe places to teach and learn. Like the princesses, meeting the challenge of maintaining the dance is essential – not doing so is too great a risk.

## References

157 Group (2013) *Curriculum redesign in further education colleges: exploring current challenges and opportunities.* Online. http://tinyurl.com/kdjtt5j (accessed 14 October 2014).

Bryan, J., and Hayes, D. (2007) 'The McDonaldisation of further education'. In Hayes, D. (ed.) *A Lecturer's Guide to Further Education.* London: McGraw-Hill.

Coffield, F. (2014) *Beyond Bulimic Learning: Improving teaching in further education.* London: Institute of Education Press.

Compass and NUT (2014) *The Interim Report of the Inquiry into a 21st Century Education System, London.* Online. www.compassonline.org.uk (accessed 14 October 2014).

Foster, A. (2005) *Realising the Potential: A review of the future role of further education colleges.* Annesley, Notts.: DfES.

Freire, P. (2004) *Pedagogy of Indignation.* Colorado: Paradigm.

— (2005) *Teachers as Cultural Workers: Letters to those who dare to teach.* Boulder, CO: Westview Press.

Hattie, J. (2003) 'Teachers Make a Difference: What is the research evidence?' Paper presented at the Australian Conference on Building Teacher Quality, Melbourne, October. Online. http://www.educationalleaders.govt.nz/Pedagogy-and-assessment/Evidence-based-leadership/Measuring-learning/Teachers-Make-a-Difference-What-is-the-Research-Evidence (accessed 1 April 2015).

hooks, b. (1994) *Teaching to Transgress: Education as the practice of freedom.* London: Routledge.

Jackson, S., and Burke P. (2007) *Reconceptualising Lifelong Learning: Feminist interventions.* London: Routledge.

Justice for Colombia (n.d.) 'End Anti-Trade-Union Violence in Colombia'. Online. www.justiceforcolombia.org/campaigns/union-rights (accessed 14 October 2014).

Lingfield, R. (2012) *Professionalism in Further Education: Final report of the Independent Review Panel* (the Lingfield review). London: BIS.

O'Grady, A. (2013) *Lifelong Learning in the UK: An introductory guide for education studies.* London: Routledge.

SAFE (n.d.) *Save Adult Further Education.* Video. Online. www.youtube.com/watch?v=qJxbWktsQEQ (accessed 14 October 2014).

UCU (n.d.) *Case study: Focus on the SAFE campaign in Liverpool.* Online. www. ucu.org.uk/1816 (accessed 14 October 2014).

Wheelahan, L. (2007) 'How competency-based training locks the working class out of powerful knowledge: A modified Bernsteinian analysis'. *British Journal of Sociology of Education*, 28 (5), 637–51.

'Sometimes when you are creative you face barriers. The support of college teachers helped me through.'

Kieran Howard

# Chapter 2

# Teaching and ideology, or why aren't we all dancing? A personal view

*Beatrix E. Groves*

'You have to love dancing to stick to it. It gives you nothing back, no manuscripts to store away, no paintings to show on walls and maybe hang in museums, no poems to be printed and sold, nothing but that single fleeting moment when you feel alive.'

(Merce Cunningham)

## Introduction

This chapter is based upon my personal experience of over 30 years of teaching, and a broad overview of the changes that have taken place in the further and adult education sector in that time. It examines the theme of conflict between doctrinaire political ideology and educational empowerment within teaching and learning. The discussion looks at the narrow instrumentalism of educational politics, and the consequent sacrifice of personal growth in learning for the greater good of an all-encompassing industrial neoliberalism. Finally, it investigates strategies which defend and encourage greater teacher autonomy, develop communities of practice and reinstate human growth as the primary domain of learning.

If it is agreed that education should involve only morally acceptable ways of teaching, then most people will immediately conclude that it should not involve indoctrination. 'Indoctrination' is a term pregnant with emotive meaning and, for most people, it is a condemnatory term. But what is its descriptive meaning? If prima facie it seems that teachers should not indoctrinate, it becomes rather important for them to know what indoctrinating is.

(Barrow and Woods, 1995: 69)

## First steps

Ironically, I hated education. My experience of it had been through the rigid regime of the Catholic schools I attended, with their all-encompassing drive for institutional success, and their sense of denial of the personal and the need-driven. My first contact with learning had been of an indoctrinating system that held little flexibility for those of us who just didn't fit the model of what a good Catholic and a good scholar should be. Learning, as I encountered it, was about serving a greater good than personal needs, and this greater good was the success of the school itself. This was rarely overtly stated by staff, but clearly implied in what were the approved – or unacceptable – choices by the pupils, achieving good O levels was at least as much about the reputation of the institution as it was about personal success in the future. My emotional needs were hemmed in by religious dogma, and my life options occluded by pressure from my teachers. Did they understand they were indoctrinating? Perhaps so, but for them faith meant more than the individual.

I first came into adult and further education as an unemployed young person in the early 1980s. Having left school with a raft of exam certificates, but with no clear idea about what I wanted to do with my life, I found I was a highly educated NEET (not in education, employment or training). I was again unequal to the socio-economic arena and at a loss as to how to be the person others wanted me to be. Hence, paradoxically, I retreated back into adult education (AE) as an escape, initially as a way of filling my time, but later seeking out the intellectual and emotional space to work out what the future held. Later I was to discover that I was not alone in this. I did not at the time realize how lucky I was, in that my second educational experience was returning-to-learn at the WEA (Workers' Educational Association). The WEA's principle of a curriculum driven by its students was a revelation to one who had been on the receiving end of education that was an ideologically closed book. This empowering liberalism became a major part of my values as I later trained to teach.

## Marching, not dancing

> The value of adult education is not solely to be measured by direct increases in earning power or productive capacity, but by the quality of life it inspires in the individual and generates for the community at large.
>
> (DES, 1973: xi)

The WEA, at the time, was still operating within the legacy of this 1973 Russell Report. For the Association, the tone of the report's preface, celebrating quality of life and community, could almost have been a mission statement. That the report was publicly welcomed by Margaret Thatcher (the then Secretary of State for Education and Science) seems supremely unexpected in retrospect. But this concealed a tacit political hostility to putting the report's modest recommendations into practice. As Paul Stanistreet put it:

> The report was submitted to Margaret Thatcher in December 1972. The reaction of Mrs Thatcher and the Conservative government that received the proposals, however, was unenthusiastic ... the oil crisis of 1973–74 and the public expenditure cuts of the 1970s made the implementation of its recommendations, which called for a 'very modest rise in total expenditure', unlikely.
>
> (Stanistreet, 2011: 8–23)

The practice of outwardly welcoming a report while practically failing to support its recommendations became a common enough experience over later years. For example, in 1997 the Kennedy Report, *Learning Works*, markedly warned that:

> Like the trickle-down theory of economics, there is a trickle-down theory of education which relies upon the notion that concentrating the bulk of educational investment on our top cohorts produces an excellence which permeates the system. For centuries, this thinking has blighted not just the British economy, but the whole of British life. It demands an urgent reappraisal.
>
> (Kennedy, 1997: 10)

Responses from the Labour Government of the time towards widening participation were enthusiastic (at least in terms of paper generated and initiatives planned with regard to vocational education). However, by 2011 the National Institute for Adult and Continuing Education (NIACE), looking back on the period, announced: 'The Institute's 2009 survey of adult participation in learning, Narrowing Participation, was a stark reminder of the challenges the sector faced. It showed a sharply widening gap between the educationally privileged and the educationally excluded' (NIACE, 2011: 22). So much for the reality of educational access. So much for the idea that a wide base for provision would gain any meaningful political support. Indeed, it is out of this history that the picture of adult and further education as the Cinderella service arises.

My own experiences mirror this process. Increasingly, the areas within which I could teach became narrowed as government reforms removed public funding streams from the liberal adult education teaching that I was part of, and redirected them to implied worthier outcomes. In most cases, growth was in skills-related training. One of the consequences of this change was a move toward a frantic defence of the liberal adult provision that remained. It was as if teaching in any field other than basic skills or Train to Gain (as it was at the time) was a hugely embarrassing quirk of an unreformed and old-fashioned mind, unable to grasp the import of the new agenda for national success. Defensiveness of this type was (and is) incredibly difficult, even though the evidence from previous decades about the efficacy of a wide-ranging curriculum, in terms of access, as previously discussed, was plentiful. The fact that providers (not just WEA, but many others) were left to justify the very existence of their educational provision, using the terminology of their critics, put them in a weak position where argument was, at best, emotively appealing but coherently wrong-footed. An unstated but major part of the problem was an underlying ideological constant, hinted at by Helena Kennedy: 'there is also growing disquiet that the new ethos has encouraged colleges not just to be businesslike but to perform as if they were businesses' (Kennedy, 1997: 3).

Kennedy's remark encapsulated an issue that I had encountered once before. That there was an underlying new faith that underpinned political management of education, and which was the tacitly accepted theme that its purpose was purely to serve the interests of political economy in a post-socialist society. All other educational experience was classed as irrelevant, or at very best something that could be paid for as a product bought by a consumer. The interpretation of widening participation, deriving from Kennedy, by the then Blairite government was slanted away from any hope of a liberal form of educational access and towards the economic benefits of qualifications: 'the aim of public funding should be to increase participation and attainment at all levels where that will provide most benefit for society. The Government recognizes the urgency of improving the nation's qualification base' (DfEE, 1998: 8). Like motherhood and apple pie this aim is undeniably sound, and few would find room to criticize it. However, when such a concept eliminates all other options, the problem of monocultural blight rears its ugly head.

Sustaining the ideological monoculture was the truism that there was a clear relationship between national educational attainment and economic success. The examples seemed very clear, especially within the East Asian economies where rapid growth came hand-in-hand with educational investment in skills. But the truism has less credibility when closely examined. Lant Pritchett famously stated in 2001 that:

> Cross national data show no association between the increases in human capital attributable to rising educational attainment of the labor force and the rate of growth of output per worker. This implies the association of educational capital growth with conventional measures of TFP (where TFP is Total Factor Productivity) is large, strongly statistically significant, and *negative*.
>
> (Pritchett, 2001: 1)

Ha-Joon Chang reiterated this message when he wrote:

> Education is valuable, but its main value is not in raising productivity. It lies in the ability to help us develop our potentials and live a more fulfilling and independent life. If we expanded education in the belief that it will make our economies richer, we will be sorely disappointed, for the link between education and national productivity is rather tenuous and complicated.
>
> (Chang, 2010: 189)

But did any government initiative take cognizance of this? If they did, it was drowned out by the ideological need to prove that free-market systems as applied to education were the sole road to a utopian future.

Once again, the needs of individuals and their search for fulfilment were subservient to a greater good: this time economic competition in a globalized world. Providers of learning were encouraged to take part in the new environment fundamentally by both direct and indirect legal and financial coercion. Nevertheless, this was too simple and blunt a tool to have a lasting change within 'the blob' of contemporary teaching (as Michael Gove describes the profession). What changed (and is still changing) was the movement of institutional cultures towards an embedded ideology-based instrumentalist process, where learning is delivered as a product and in which that product only has value to the extent that it makes individuals job-ready for whatever employment is available at the time. To me, this seems an all too familiar situation, frighteningly redolent of the Fordian choices of my educational youth. But what makes matters worse is the universalization of such cultures, across educational providers, as pragmatic cost-of-survival in the post-historic era. As Fukuyama predicted: 'The triumph of the West, of the Western idea, is evident first of all in the total exhaustion of viable systematic alternatives to Western liberalism' (1989: 1). The emphasis in the

UK education sector is not so much on a euphemistic liberalism (which is interpreted through the notion of consumerist choice) but in the 'exhaustion of viable systematic alternatives' (ibid.)

The surprise is not that this has come to pass, but that so many of my colleagues have taken on board the new culture as if it were a normative state of affairs. Teachers may question how things are done (in terms of pay and conditions, for example) but rarely target the underpinning values from which these issues have arisen. The narrowing possibilities for action within the curriculum on offer in effect means that many of us working within the sector are complicit in an indoctrination process (if not indoctrination itself) in which the ideological regime goes unquestioned in our day-to-day work. I am not immune to this. In my own practice I find myself compromising on a daily basis as I scramble for work, taking on board issues that I would have found anathema not so long ago, coupled to an ever-decreasing range of opportunities for unconstrained discourse with my colleagues. Stanley Milgram made plain the need for such contact some 40 years ago when he voiced his warning about the impact of monocultural authority systems. 'When an individual wishes to stand in opposition to authority, the mutual support provided by men for each other is the strongest bulwark we have against the excesses of authority' (Milgram, 1974: 121). But as work has become more intense, chances to discuss educational matters in a community of practice setting have become fleeting. This is to the extent that many of us find ourselves completely isolated in our jobs and, consequently, also our praxis. Viable systematic alternatives to the current teaching-learning situation do exist, but the chance to engage with them is fleeting, and even when this happens they are seen as secondary to the practicalities of staying in a job.

## The problems of learning to dance

It might be said that learning to dance, when the only dance that there has been is marching in step, is a slow and sometimes painful process. But if 'the structure does not permit dialogue the structure must be changed' (Freire, 1972: 69), and it is only through evolving new and powerful structures that a dialectical democracy, supporting communities of practice (or discovery), can come into being.

It may seem impossible to combat the effects of an all-pervading culture where there is little room for action, and little opportunity for organization. But it seems to me that the answer is not in restating the problems of current educational policy yet again. Such a strategy has a cathartic effect for the reader and writer alike, but does little to encourage action. Indeed, it can paint such an overwhelming picture of adversity that most teachers will shrug their shoulders in despair and continue to knuckle down to the immediate chores they have to hand.

Firstly, what is proposed is the development of a positive alternative ideology that counteracts the existing dominant culture from the bottom upward, providing greater access to a public sphere of debate which avoids the distortions of the political economy. This means the creation of new public organizations that are a forum for teachers within the post-compulsory sector, owned and run by the teachers themselves and without the restrictive practices of their predecessors. Trade unions themselves cannot fulfil this role. They have a specialized job to do within the traditional domain of terms, conditions and pay, but their alliance with party politics means their influence is not always completely benign.

Such organs as the Institute for Learning (IfL) have distinctly failed either to legitimately represent the bulk of educators or to find a robust voice that adequately speaks in a challenging fashion about government policy and the underpinning ideology it represents. Much though the Institute yearned to fill this role, its flirtations with authority (both formal and informal) meant that its credibility was lost long before it became a truly independent body. What is needed now is a new self-organized free association of teachers in FE and AE, which sustains a public sphere for educational debate and which takes on board three guiding principles, well known from Habermas's diagnosis of public discourse in the early 1960s:

- a disregard of status (open to all teachers, irrespective of their background or experience)
- a domain of common concern (interested purely in the broad impact of teaching, its praxis and social-political context)
- inclusivity (bringing on board a diverse range of views, supporting a dialectical democracy that establishes a culture of openness and critical analysis as a foundational value).

(Habermas, 1989: 36)

That there is potential for a new organization seems clear. Membership of IfL was substantial and wide-based (even though its impact on members was questionable) and loyalty to the Institute was strong among its core old-timers. The Education and Training Foundation (ETF) cannot fulfil this role, as it is clearly an employer-based body. Its interests lie elsewhere. But a new body with a strong consciousness of ideological issues could be an attractive proposition for many working in the sector.

Secondly, those of us working in initial teacher education (ITE) need to take a strong responsibility to ensure that analytic skills are taught as part of the training of new FE and AE teachers. Current ITE curriculum at the award and certificate levels is seriously limited to practical matters of teaching. Much is studied around the role of teaching (in a conventionalized sense), the methodology, assessment processes and institutional context, etc. But all of this leans towards a very limited and packaged range of actions which embody the notion that teaching is purely about input–output processes (raw bodies in, educated people out) that can be managed via constant punitive monitoring. Very little, if anything, is said about the politics of education (other than the facts of legal change) or about the philosophy of education and learning. Critical reasoning skills are vital to the capacity of teachers to engage with their students in the context of their lives and communities. Similarly they are vital to an emergence of teacher autonomy, with all that implies for thoroughgoing praxis and its potential aim: the fulfilment of lives within a just and open society.

Teacher educators need to take on the vital role of standing fast for widening the options taught within ITE. They need to find time within their schemes of work to rebalance instrumentalism with an empowering approach that allows new teachers to stake a claim for the wider needs of their students and themselves. As a teacher educator myself, I am more than a little aware of the role this work plays, and the constant struggle to broaden students' horizons beyond the immediate and the pragmatic. Wriggle-room is scarce within timetables, but worth pursuing as a matter of priority.

Thirdly, James Park's report for DEMOS entitled Detoxifying School Accountability makes the case for multi-perspective inspection over current quality monitoring within education:

> The core belief of this [current] system is that school leaders, and the teams of people who work with them, cannot be trusted to assess the strengths and weaknesses of their organizations, or to develop strategies for making their schools even better. This can only be done under the supervision of outsiders.
>
> (Park, 2013: 43)

Though this report discussed the schools system only, it hit upon a notion that was familiar to teachers within FE and AE, namely the anxieties created by OFSTED visits and graded observation of teaching and learning (OTL) systems performed by providers on their own staff. That these procedures are a dubious guarantee of teaching quality is discussed at length by Park (and others, for example Coffield, 2012), and furthermore they indicate the serious negative impact such methods have on teacher confidence, professionalism, autonomy and imagination. Clearly, such damage does have a price, and that price is unwillingness for educators to step outside the boundaries of what is safely orthodox. This creates a kind of cultural indoctrination: what is safe is rewarded by good grades; what is unsafe (whatever that arbitrarily might mean) is punished by employment capability procedures. That many, if not all, teachers in FE and AE find this system abhorrent takes little imagination to understand. That there is little rebellion against its exigencies is more surprising, but it is likely to be an indicator of an enculturated Somme mentality. For most the anxiety is a normalized (and therefore expected) condition of the working regime. The shelling is ameliorated by it being a common factor, experienced by all the troops.

Yet this situation points towards another rallying point for collective action. The unpopularity of unnecessarily stressful working conditions (and particularly when, as Park has indicated, there are other methods of quality monitoring), the divisive, costly and overly bureaucratic procedures, and the culture of fear they engender, all provide a focus for challenging one dynamic of the dominant monoculture. Teachers themselves should be encouraged to analyse collectively what makes for better teaching and learning, and this means both actively resisting punitive monitoring and demanding time within the working week for collegiate sharing of good practice. This has been a common theme in meetings and conferences I have attended over the past five years, and repeatedly the plea has been 'we don't have enough time'. The rallying point for change here, however, is in building active communities of practice that involve contact and sharing not simply because this removes fear, but because it is an effective and efficient way of raising standards and encouraging innovation.

## A last waltz

One of my favourite quotes is from the novel *The Once and Future King* by T.H. White. In this tale of the life of King Arthur, Merlin gives a wise summary of his views on learning to his young pupil. It is something I regularly pass on to my students:

> You may grow old and trembling in your anatomies, you may lie
> awake at night listening to the disorder of your veins, you may
> miss your only love, you may see the world about you devastated
> by evil lunatics, or know your honour trampled in the sewer of

baser minds. There is only one thing for it then – to learn. Learn why the world wags and what wags it.

(White, 1958: 183)

The emphasis Merlin passes on to Wart (Arthur to be) is not the purity of learning as a good thing in itself, nor the glory of learning for the sake of academic achievement nor the acquisition of appropriate skills to be a good king, but the determining factor that makes learning valuable: why the world wags and what wags it.

Our world grows ever more complex, and not only in technological terms. The matter of life, how it may be lived and with what existential purpose, nags at us every day. Political decision making seems more distant than ever. The complex structural regimes that support such systems make individual participation seem marginal or pointless. Our knowledge sources are more extensive than at any time in history, and yet we find ourselves feeling less well informed and less in control than ever. We sometimes drown in information. And throughout this, our educational systems are criticized in the media for not serving the needs of the new world order. Teachers find themselves facing the brunt of ideologies that respond with greater control measures, their skills and efforts regularly vilified and reformed.

But Merlin's advice to Wart still applies, and motivates me in what I do in teaching and learning. It is holding on to such values that makes teaching worth pursuing and underpins the partnerships built up between student and teacher as learning takes place. Such waltzes are still worth dancing, both now and in the future.

## References

Barrow, R., and Woods, R. (1995) *An Introduction to Philosophy of Education.* 3rd ed. London: Routledge.

Chang, H. (2010) *23 Things They Don't Tell You About Capitalism.* London: Penguin Books.

Coffield, F. (2012) 'To grade or not to grade'. *Adults Learning*, 23 (4), 38–9.

DES (1973) *Adult Education: A plan for development* (the Russell Report). London: HMSO.

DfEE (1998) *Further Education for the New Millennium: Response to the Kennedy Report.* London: DfEE.

Freire, P. (1972) *Pedagogy of the Oppressed.* Harmondsworth: Penguin Books.

Fukuyama, F. (1989) 'The end of history?' *The National Interest*, 16 (4), 3–18.

Habermas, J. (1989) *The Structural Transformation of the Public Sphere: An inquiry into a category of bourgeois society.* Cambridge, MA: MIT Press.

Kennedy, H. (1997) *Learning Works: Widening participation in further education.* London: FEFC.

Milgram, S. (1974) *Obedience to Authority.* New York: Harper & Row.

NIACE (2011) *Narrowing Participation for Adults: The NIACE 2009 survey on Adult Participation in Learning.* Leicester: NIACE.

Park, J. (2013) *Detoxifying School Accountability: The case for multi-perspective inspection.* London: DEMOS.

Pritchett, L. (2001) 'Where has all the education gone?' *World Bank Economic Review*, 15 (3), 367–91.

Stanistreet, P. (2011) 'The Learning Age and After'. *Adults Learning*, 22 (8), 8–23.

White, T.H. (1958) *The Once and Future King.* London: Penguin Books.

'FE was a doorway to fulfil my passion for self-expression, and a stepping stone to international training and professional touring. It was a seed that has allowed me to continue growing through my world-dance company as a teacher, mentor and motivator.'

Ithalia Forel

# Chapter 3

# Critical pedagogy in FE
*Rebecca Maxted*

'There are movements which impinge upon the nerves with a strength that is incomparable, for movement has power to stir the senses and emotions, unique in itself. This is the dancer's justification for being, and his reason for searching further for deeper aspects of his art.'

(Doris Humphrey)

This chapter focuses upon the practice of critical pedagogy in FE in England and outlines the ways in which many of the teachers within the FE sector are making a conscious and determined effort to preserve what they see as real education within the context of a neoliberal, marketized education system. It is based on semi-structured interviews undertaken in 2010–12 with ten such teachers in colleges in the north of England. Participants described their understandings of critical pedagogy and neoliberalism and went on to outline the political and ethical discourses within which they situated themselves and from which they drew inspiration. They described how this inspiration translates into critical pedagogy in the classroom; how theoretical influences help them to choreograph their professional lives and, thus, how they manage to keep dancing. Some participants also described how life experiences have led them to support critical approaches in education as a means of working towards social justice and increased opportunities for their students, while others described their views on broader political and social changes needed outside the classroom.

The concept of critical pedagogy is multivalent, used by critical race theorists, Marxists, neo-Marxists, feminists, Foucauldians, queer theorists and others. I am, however, primarily interested in ways in which educators use critical pedagogy to question or subvert the hegemony of neoliberalism and the policies and view of human nature it promotes, as well as the individualistic ontological and epistemological assumptions it rests upon.

Terms such as critical education and social justice have to some extent been recuperated by hegemonic neoliberalism so it was difficult to be certain whether or not the teachers who described their own pedagogy as critical were using the term in the Freirean sense. There is considerable potential for ideological confusion in this regard (Gur-Ze'ev *et al.*, 2001;

Rizvi and Lingard, 2010). This re-articulation or recuperation of concepts under neoliberalism brings with it particular difficulties of interpretation, operationalization of concepts and selection of a purposive sample. Are there any teachers who would not claim to be working in the interests of justice and equality? The meaning of the terms changes in different ideological contexts. I asked respondents to explain their understanding of critical education precisely in order to check how they understood the concept.

Participants showed a sophisticated and nuanced understanding of the concept. One described the way in which critical pedagogy encourages students to question social institutions and norms, including the education system itself:

> It's continually reflective of not only your own practice but of the purposes of education and learning – not only in the context of students themselves but in the context of society as a whole. And how society views education and how the governmental administrative structures organize education.

Another participant explained:

> It's teaching in a way that you criticize the power structures and orthodoxies and hegemony. A kind of counter-hegemonic project.

One participant elaborated upon the moral duty to empower students through raising their awareness of social structures and their impact on students' lives. For her, critical pedagogy included the requirement to:

> Educate them about why the curriculum is like it is … empower them so that they can be good people, so that they can take part in society, take part in their own life, be in charge of their own destiny. So they can understand what's happening around them and why it's happening around them. Just make sure that they are aware of the wider social implications of the framework, of the education that they're taking part in.

For others, critical pedagogy went beyond consciousness raising and involved practical action too:

> It's creating an awareness of how those taken-for-granted ideas are probably not in everyone's best interests. And not necessarily just an awareness – but it's about, now that we're aware, what can we do to change and challenge those things?

Respondents also had a profound understanding of neoliberalism and its effects on the education system. Their view was that there has been an intensification over the last two decades of policies supporting marketization, in line with the neoliberal agenda. This includes, in FE, the removal of colleges from local authority control, the proliferation of league tables, the perceived fragmentation and deracination of knowledge and an emphasis on targets and outcomes rather than individuals.

One respondent said that neoliberalism was life-denying and nihilist:

> It justifies inequality and over-rationalization for the sake of unnecessary and potentially disastrous productivity. Values aren't recognized. They disappear from people's thinking and people's discourse. Over-rationalization is the use of instrumental reason to control life in as many aspects as possible. It makes me think of Freud's idea of the death instinct, *thanatos*, where you want to get everything under control. We want everything under control, and we can't actually cope with life. You know, life isn't controllable. All the best aspects of life are uncontrollable. They're sort of spontaneous – that's what's so wonderful about them – they're miracles, if you like, but we don't, we want to control miracles. I think neoliberalism is just sort of more and more control in the interests of productivity.

Another interviewee agreed that the values of neoliberalism are reductionist:

> Everything has to be viewed in terms of market relationships and market relationships are the mechanism for achieving any desired outcome in society or in economic or educational terms. Not only is the market the thing through which anything desirable can be achieved, but nothing that is not marketized is desirable.

Many participants pointed out that, in their view, the current marketized education system was dehumanizing, anti-personal and anti-individualist.

Contrasts were drawn between an insular, self-referential, self-perpetuating system which might expect students to obey rules for their own sake and which would deliberately obscure the truth of the students' situation (and which enabled less critical teachers to assume for themselves some kind of status as bearers of privileged knowledge) and a critical desire to cast as much light as possible on all kinds of situations, including and most obviously the education system itself, in order to educate students in meaningful ways. One respondent said:

> Students say, 'Why do we have to do this? Why do we have to do the other?' I've tried giving them the spin – oh, it's good, it will help you in life – but then eventually, I'll just tell them the truth and say, 'Look, you have to do this because then we get the funding for A, B and C.' At managers' meetings, they'll say, 'Don't let students know this.' But it's dishonest and manipulative, not to let students know. Why would you not? I know I shouldn't say it, but I can't resist, because it's the truth.

Nearly all the participants articulated a strong desire for social justice. This seemed to them a natural and inescapable moral stance, which had led them to become educators in the first place. Their distress at finding themselves within an education system that was, as they saw it, at best uninterested in social justice and, at worst, the main state apparatus by which inequality is maintained and reproduced, resulted in extreme cognitive dissonance and profound moral unease.

Some participants wanted to work towards social justice because their own class backgrounds had given them direct insights into injustice and inequality. One teacher described how her working-class background, interpreted in the light of an A level sociology textbook illustration, fired her desire to work for social justice through education:

> One of the sociology textbooks has a section introducing Marxism – or maybe it's illustrating the good points of functionalism. It's like a factory, and it shows the little people on factory lines, and the posh ones go here and the not-so-posh ones go down there. I was brought up on a council estate in Blackburn. I think back to my secondary modern, because I failed the grammar tests. I remember our teachers always saying to us, because we weren't conforming, 'You'll get nowhere in life. You'll work behind a bacon counter.' One of my friends really wanted to do a PhD in psychology, and the teacher said to her, 'Somebody who goes to a secondary modern can't do a PhD.' And she's just finished it now. She phoned [the school in question] and told them about it. That's what inspires me, to think that anybody, given the choice and the right opportunity, can do anything that they want to do, but some people are more disadvantaged than others. If you just brainwash them with this idea that it's equal opportunities – you have this curriculum, and equal opportunity – well, that's a load of crap. They haven't got an equal opportunity. That's what makes me let people know what the situation is.

Another participant had experienced how life chances and opportunities had changed for her according to her economic status at different points in her life. This experience had deeply shocked her and exposed, for her, the myth of meritocracy. She said:

> I left home at 20 and found myself on my own. I was very lucky that I had some good friends and we all supported each other. It was a case of, 'Who's got a fiver?', and we're spending that one this week! And if somebody had bread and somebody else had meat, well then, we all joined together and we had a feast. It seemed so simple, that if people work together and support each other, things work well. I then went on to have a really good marriage and it made an incredible difference to what I was able to achieve, because I had the safety net of this marriage and relative financial security. It gave me the freedom to be able to return to education. It just seems so bizarre to me that whether or not you can be educated depends on where you start out. Because if I were still on my own as a single parent, there is no way I would have been able to afford to stop working, to go back to college. It just wouldn't have happened. Unfair sounds such a baby word, doesn't it? But I haven't got a stronger word that we can use. The thing is, it's absolutely despicable.

Participants expressed great unease about the impact of neoliberalism on education, saying that it had resulted in what they saw as a 'tick box' culture where knowledge is fragmented and atomized into meaningless lists. So reductive is this approach that some teachers felt that what they were teaching was nothing more than a convenient homeopathic package of information that had been diluted to such an extent that any original significance had been lost (and, perhaps, the homeopathic remedy discouraged the students from accessing any real remedy for ignorance). One said:

> What we're pushed into doing, is teaching just to get an exam result. And I even find myself occasionally saying – for our exam purposes, this is what this means but it's not really true. I don't like myself saying it. For example, someone might say something interesting about whether Marxists might want to use unstructured interviews! Actually, I think often they would! But according to A levels, Marxists are positivists, so …

Many participants were critical of what they saw as over-assessment of students within a system that fostered and depended upon the surveillance and control of students and staff alike:

> There's such a culture of inspection and checking and auditing and systems that it's all about the system and not about the reality. That's a classic conflict, because people want to check that the right thing is being done, but in the end the systems for checking become more important than other things.

Several pointed out that this change in emphasis had fundamentally altered relationships between staff and students and that the distance between staff and students had increased and this made it difficult to teach in critical ways. One or two participants spoke regretfully about the effects of the changed environment on the students. One said that the impact of neoliberal education policies was to 'fragment personalities until they become just bearers of grades'.

This concern for results rather than people was a key theme for many participants who felt that students were being manipulated by a system that didn't operate in their best interests. One pointed out that:

> It doesn't support individualization. OFSTED inspections talk about being able to differentiate for learners, but the system doesn't support that. You can't differentiate fully if everyone has the same outcomes, the same boxes that have to be ticked in the same time frame.

Several participants were very critical of what they saw as a bankrupt utilitarian moral stance underpinning the wholesale sacrifice of personalities on the altar of increased productivity:

> Nothing is of value which can't be measured. It's an obsessive driving-through of utilitarianism in a way in which people do not actually recognize what it is. The idea that utilitarianism is actually unchallengeable common sense, whereas it is a very explicit philosophical concept and structure which has been subject to very rigorous criticism. You need to say, this is utilitarianism and this is why it's rubbish. We need to be absolutely upfront here – you know, name it for what it is, and not let people assume that it is a natural state of things. It isn't – it is a very distinct, clear and identifiable philosophical, administrative position.

The students were very critical of managerialist culture and felt that the utilitarian emphasis was strongly upheld by a management class which had taken control of education in the last two or three decades. Managers, said some, didn't even realize that education might be approached in other ways – hence the above participant's emphasis upon the need to expose the utilitarian philosophical underpinnings of managerialism. However, those who had experience of working in management seemed to feel equally despondent and helpless in the face of a system at odds with their own values:

> One of the reasons why I want to quit the divisional manager job is that I go home at night thinking, 'God, you're an arse. So-and-so is really stressed and you're making them more stressed, and you have to make them more stressed to achieve A, B, and C.'

## Solutions

What does critical pedagogy look like in practice? Some participants felt that they didn't use particular techniques and that their critical pedagogy was more about attitude, personality or values. One said:

> I'm not sure I've devised any specific activities. Erich Fromm says that teachers' main influence on people, is them, their person, their being, if you like. It's a typical existentialist approach. The way you are. I don't think you can be criticizing inequality if you are craving status and climbing the career ladder. There's also not focusing all the time on exams – let's say if you occasionally do a lesson on something that's in the news, even though it's got nothing to do with the syllabus. Somebody brings something up, nothing to do with the syllabus but it's important, just stop, get on with it ... If you're lucky enough to have students like that, it's worth stimulating that, and that gets across the message that exams aren't that important, league tables aren't that important, you know, because other things are more important. But a lot of teachers are scared to do it.

A number of other participants also mentioned the importance of going off-piste and not teaching always to the exam; several espoused the view that this was often disconcerting for teachers. Others stressed the significance of extra-curricular activities, including trips. Some teachers linked such activities to the development of the students' personalities. One said:

> Critical pedagogy is actually – how can we serve the people who come? Then you develop the personality. You look at the

personality in terms of the current situation. How do you develop it? One problem is that a lot of teachers feel isolated and scared about innovating.

Many of the teachers talked about the central importance of encouraging students to question everything and to consider and evaluate as many views as possible. The critical teacher's role was to open up possibilities for students rather than narrowing them down:

> Our role as teachers is to be a conduit. If that is narrowing, and you're saying, see things through this lens and you can't look beyond it, then you're a barrier between the student and stuff they could find out. Being a critical teacher is adding something to the process rather than taking something away. You know, have you thought about this, have you questioned it? Do you think that actually is what it says it is? Could there be another reason why this exists? Could there be another reason why people say this? And so that's what I think we're there for, really.

Many teachers questioned the dominant view in their colleges that staff should remain objective and not share their own opinions; one teacher in particular thought that critical pedagogy included encouraging students to critique the views of the teachers, as a good route into academic debate:

> I made a decision that I'd just tell students where I was coming from, so that they could be critical of me. What I think it does mean is that you can have pretty strong debates and discussion and some people will be prepared to give their views if they think that you're prepared to give your views.

Several participants related this use of critical questioning to the importance of empowerment and honesty. Encouraging students to see as much as possible, in a kind of cubist approach to knowledge, was felt to be central to critical pedagogy. There was clearly a connection here between distaste for fragmentation – seen as partial, dishonest and disempowering – and a desire to shine as many lights as possible on the subject at hand. Several respondents mentioned their wish to connect with other disciplines in order to cast more light on particular subjects, but found that there was seldom time to go beyond what was needed for the exam.

The participants felt indignant about a system that encouraged them to obscure the truth from students and were determined to allow students to discover as many truths and perspectives as possible, the better to understand their own lives. One teacher said this approach involved 'treating students as equals'; another felt it involved sharing one's own journey of critical inquiry.

Other teachers mentioned how useful particular disciplines, such as sociology, were in helping students to develop critical approaches. However, one teacher commented that teaching about critical subjects didn't necessarily mean that one was deploying critical pedagogy. Indeed, the unquestioning presentation of a critical perspective as a choice among many may serve to neuter that perspective and result in its recuperation into the hegemonic framework:

> Obviously, in sociology, you're constantly talking about critics. But that isn't in itself critical pedagogy – to say, this is what Marx thinks, this is what Foucault thinks, that's not critical pedagogy.

Method counts more than content in the practice of critical pedagogy. In this respect, four teachers mentioned the need to give students some time to reflect and consider their opinions – time and silence, in fact, in which to allow the mind to work at a deeper level than that required by the bite-size sound-bite exam culture.

Several respondents found it helpful to address the wider context in which the education system is situated, recognizing that a change of policy environment might actually be the most helpful thing possible in facilitating the development of critical pedagogy:

> It's got to be a lot wider than schools. I'd like to adapt Marx, saying the people get the government they deserve – I'd say, you get the education system you deserve as well. So the challenging doesn't happen just in classrooms, it happens constantly, wherever you are. Well, obviously, you don't want to become a bore, but it's got to be challenged wherever you find it. Society doesn't end at the classroom walls.

Another spoke passionately about the need for political reform but cautioned that, 'any counter-reaction to it will have to think about not restoring the *status quo ante*'. Instead, this teacher wanted to see a firm and broad development of local accountability, via democratically elected local education boards, enabling genuine critical dialogue about curricula and policy.

All the teachers interviewed were determined to carry on using critical pedagogy in the classroom, though for some this meant that they were leaving the FE sector and looking for work elsewhere. Several interviewees spoke of the professional isolation and sense of embattlement experienced by those who seek to educate in this way; these interviewees clearly wished to take action to erode that sense of professional loneliness and contribute towards practical solutions that help to facilitate the renewed emphasis upon criticality in education. One said:

> I do feel quite isolated, actually, quite lonely, so access to other people who are using critical pedagogy would be great.

Other interviewees described their approach as 'counter-hegemonic' and expressed a desire to work with others in some kind of counter-hegemonic bloc, drawing in one case upon Avis's insight that:

> Educational struggles need to be lodged within a social movement that seeks to undermine oppressive and exploitative relations in order to extend social justice and democracy throughout society.
>
> (Avis, 2007: 165)

## Conclusion

FE can still be a site of transformative education; many of those who work within the sector do so because of the sector's potential as an engine of social mobility. It is important that critical educators in FE neither give up nor try simply to maintain a professional life as anachronistic curiosities in spaces round the edges of the neoliberal advance. Education, of course, is the site of cultural transmission of norms and values but those educators who believe that the norms and values, transmitted under neoliberalism are reductive, ignoble and exploitative can reclaim space for alternative views through determined collaborative action supported by theoretical analysis. As Avis has observed:

> If education is thought of as a site of struggle, one in which inequality is produced, interventions within the classroom may serve to interrupt this process. In this way attempts to transform learning cultures within further education may have a subversive edge. After all it would be risible to evacuate the classroom, or indeed education, as a site of struggle.
>
> (Avis, 2007: 159–60)

It is difficult to find spaces to continue this struggle, given the diktats of funding and the culture of performativity and instrumentalism within English FE. This chapter has outlined some ways in which it is being done, alongside considerations of why it ought to be done. Examples given of existing critical practices and instances where critical spaces are being opened up may be adapted and transferred to other contexts. In this respect, the establishment of a critical education forum in FE would be of great practical use and support.

If the princesses are to keep dancing despite their restrictions, and if they are to dance beyond those restrictions, further research on critical pedagogy in FE might be helpful. Examination of the theoretical underpinnings of these teachers' pedagogical stances begins to illuminate how counter-hegemonic knowledge is produced and sustained. This new knowledge may, in turn, translate into practices that act as critical wedges to open up and expand spaces in which critical educators, and their students, can dance more freely.

## References

Avis, J. (2007) *Education, Policy and Social Justice: Learning and skills.* London: Continuum.

Gur-Ze'ev, I., Masschelein, J., and Blake, N. (2001) 'Reflectivity, reflection and counter-education'. *Studies in Philosophy and Education,* 20 (2), 93–106.

Rizvi, F., and Lingard, B. (2010) *Globalizing Education Policy.* London: Routledge.

## Further reading

Apple, M., Au, W., and Gandin, L. (2009) *The Routledge International Handbook of Critical Education.* London: Routledge.

Kincheloe, J. (2008) *Knowledge and Critical Pedagogy: An introduction.* Montreal: Springer.

McLaren, P. (2001) 'Che Guevara, Paulo Freire, and the politics of hope: Reclaiming critical pedagogy'. *Cultural Studies: Critical Methodologies,* 1 (1), 108–31.

Macrine, S., McLaren, P., and Hill, D. (2010) *Revolutionizing pedagogy: Education for social justice within and beyond global neo-liberalism.* Basingstoke: Palgrave Macmillan.

Olssen, M. (2006) 'Understanding the mechanisms of neoliberal control: Lifelong learning, flexibility and knowledge capitalism'. *International Journal of Lifelong Education,* 25 (3), 213–30.

Wrigley, T., Lingard, B., and Thomson, P. (2012) 'Pedagogies of transformation: Keeping hope alive in troubled times'. *Critical Studies in Education,* 53 (1), 95–108.

'FE opened doors of knowledge for me, into a new exciting world
that I didn't realize I would learn to love.'

Phillip David Ashby

# Chapter 4

# Frivolity as resistance?

What do the dancing princesses and their shoes that were danced to pieces tell us about risk taking and the potential for pedagogic bungee jumping in FE classrooms?

## *Julie Hughes*

'*Dance first. Think later. It's the natural order.*'

(Samuel Beckett)

The will to live in creative spaces and their associated temporal rhythms require positive courage; the courage to live in the future and take on tasks that have to be uncertain as to their outcomes.

(Barnett, 2010: 81)

A: I needed to 'face my fears and address them'.

C: But, and this is a big but for me, I have felt some loss of control.

The linguistic slippage in the title of the Grimms' story, 'The Twelve Dancing Princess *or* The Worn Out Dancing Shoes *or* The Shoes That Were Danced To Pieces' *might* be read as a reframing of the narrative and its moral impulses, which require the reader to be mindful of the gap and of the need to tackle the border issues (Bolton, 2001: xvi). The transcription, curation and editing of the fairy tales by the Brothers Grimm allows us to use their fabrication as a lens to consider the actions of the participants (Luke, 1982). Thus, in the title shifts it could be argued that the passive or sleeping princesses are reconfigured as agents who joyfully dance their shoes to pieces transgressing their social roles and responsibilities. Nevertheless, the frivolity of the dance is the princesses' downfall and their father's fear of the frivolous and his need to contain their dancing leads to them becoming the *un*dancing princesses with the eldest married off, therefore reinforcing appropriate social codes and behaviours.

Just as the title of the compilation of Grimms' stories might be interpreted as 'for children and the household' (Luke, 1982: 9), so the princesses' actions might be read as an illustration, albeit temporary, of the potential for transgressive and critical mischief making, or for frivolity. Following Maclure's proposition that frivolity is 'an ethical, critical and practical response to contemporary educational policy discourses' (2005: 2), this chapter draws upon staff and student narratives, such as A and C quoted above, concerning their use of technology to consider persistence in Barnett's (2007: 2) terms, as effort and even anxiety, and how in a period of risk aversion, accountability and consumerism, teachers and their learners maintain their will to learn, 'to dance'. The *will* to learn, to take risks, to be frivolous with technology, is of crucial significance, as the past two years have seen an acceleration of policy in regard to workforce development in the FE sector, which will be discussed below.

The taking of risks, taking part in the dance, resonates with Barnett's paralleling between the acts of bungee jumping and learning. As learning, and I will argue teaching, in the FE sector:

> [...] calls for courage on the part of the learner/*teacher* and a will to leap into a kind of void. There is bound to be uncertainty. A pedagogy of air ... opens up spaces and calls for a will to learn ... even amid uncertainty ... it is just possible that the learner/*teacher* may come into a new mode of being.
>
> (Barnett, 2007: 1)

This potential new mode is underpinned by participation rather than acquisition metaphors for learning (Coffield, 2008) and characterizes education as dialogue. It is the pursuit of meaningful collaboration and participation supported by technology, as risk and frivolity, which this chapter will explore.

Coffield (ibid.: 7), reflecting common fears about the use of technology in education, quotes Skinner from the 1960s, who powerfully argued: 'any teacher who can be replaced by a computer, should be'. The nuances of the culture-shifts required for 'blending' education through technology are beautifully illustrated by Coffield's (ibid.: 36) reference to Alexander's reiteration of the role of democratic dialogue in education which is, 'a meeting of minds and ideas as well as of voices; and it is therefore mediated through text, internet and computer screen as well as through face-to-face interaction'. It is the mediation that may be perceived as the biggest threat and risk. In a standardized education culture that relies upon visible face-to-face attendance and registration, the blend of online activity may be rendered invisible and therefore not valuable in the same way as the presence of teachers and learners in face-to-face classrooms.

There is a myth that blending the curriculum is necessarily a cheaper option. As Garrison and Anderson (2003) demonstrated, however, the pedagogic needs of a blended learning community of inquiry require a different type of teaching presence (not a different type of teacher *per se*).

This involves planning and design of educational interactions that develop what they term both social and cognitive presences. Garrison and Anderson propose a dialogue-based, participatory approach to the use of technology. This chapter examines the issues when adopting this approach with new and experienced teachers engaging in professional learning programmes.

Facer's claim that 'education is a site in which visions of the future proliferate' (2011: 1) is a poignant one as teacher education and continuing professional development (CPD) for the lifelong sector in the UK is under increasing intervention, scrutiny and contraction. There have been mixed messages from government with regard to workforce development, professional standards and the increasing need for the FE sector to engage with technology in a pedagogically informed manner.

Investment in teacher time and space for innovation and creativity are crucial to the success of workforce developments, yet historically investment has been driven by top-down policy making and technological determinism (de Freitas and Jameson, 2012). This misalignment between the remote policy maker and the frontline of the classroom is widening and 'the lack of alignment of educational policies both with learning theory and with empirical evidence of "what works" in education explains, at least in part, why educational policy has been so unsuccessful at bridging the divide' (ibid.: 10). The focus upon hardware purchase and budgets has resulted in 'excellent examples of pedagogic practice in E-learning [which] have tended to be restricted to a relatively small number of experts ... pockets of excellence ... we would say "Freda and Charlie in the Shed syndrome" with little ability to be broadened out to the widest communities' (ibid.).

Laurillard (2013: 13) similarly identified that 'we need investment not only in technology but also in teaching as a "design science", i.e. teachers building on each other's best ideas, experimenting, innovating, testing, improving and exchanging the optimal ways of using learning technologies'. Despite the identification of the need for CPD there has been a sectoral focus upon technological products, resources and data collection activity, supported by technology, and no mention of the potential for social interaction, dialogue and teacher design opportunities. Conole and Alevizou's (2010: 43) research into HE teachers' use of technology found that teachers 'draw on past experience rather than actual empirical evidence and research literature. Despite the benefits and need for more scholarly activities, there is little evidence that this actually occurs.' They argue that a knowing and scholarly approach is necessary for the potential of technologies to be realized and to create opportunities for educators to be 'co-innovators in understanding the key possibilities in the relationship between technology and pedagogy, leading towards a co-evolved professional knowledge base that stems from reflective practices that are mediated and shared; a practice that feeds into the development of curricular designs that can actualize educational visions' (ibid.: 43).

Facer's (2011) recognition of how technologies may shape the world through use and re-appropriation is significant if teachers are to have a stake in the shaping of learning and teaching. If learning is perceived as acquisition, this 'tends to assume that learning is individual; that it is the direct result of teaching which is seen as a simple, technical process' (Coffield, 2008: 17). It was therefore refreshing from both a policy and practitioner perspective to receive the recommendations of the Further Education Learning Technology Action Group (FELTAG) in 2014. FELTAG was formed by the Minister of State for FE and Skills in 2013 to consider paths forward to a digital future in the sector. Its position statement in the Executive Summary (FELTAG, 2014: 4) states that 'digital technology was not the end goal in itself, Government cannot, and should not, provide all the answers and ownership by the FE sector of FELTAG's outcomes is key.' The report's recommendations are sector wide and at the time of writing their status is still unclear. What is significant, however, is that the group that produced the report will continue as the cross-sector Education Technology Action Group (ETAG).

FELTAG's statement on the capacity of the FE workforce is plain (2014: 5): 'the entire workforce has to be brought up to speed to fully understand the potential of learning technologies', which needs 'significant investment in the knowledge, skills and understanding of the learning technologies potential among policy-makers, governors, principals, seniors and middle management, teachers and support staff'. The report identifies the prevalence of earlier technological determinism as it recommends that, 'continuous professional development for teachers needs to be considered when purchasing any capital expenditure for learning technology' (ibid.). This shift away from hardware and software to the development needs of teachers and the workforce in its entirety is noteworthy.

Unlike the deficit model of staff attitude and experience presented by the earlier Whitehead review (2013), FELTAG offers a more nuanced and evidence-informed view of practitioners and managers and their perspectives on the use of learning technologies. The report identifies examples of a growing trend of innovative initiatives instigated by individuals, supported by their peers. FELTAG's survey of practitioners found that their respondents were less fearful than the workforce portrayed by Whitehead, who were more curious and more likely to experiment with 'their personal digital technology experience and apply this to the circumstances of their learners' (FELTAG, 2014: 13). The report recorded evidence of increasing confidence and capability among some practitioners but the means to share these ideas and developments is missing at every level.

Managers' responses to FELTAG's survey echo the arguments outlined above, citing a lack of funding to purchase products and to then support practice development in the workforce. Despite recent changes to funding learning, providers 'will shy away from fully exploiting digital technology in their operations until funding methodologies are perceived to be supportive of digital technology-supported learning' (ibid.: 14). Staff compliance with policy drivers, such as monitoring student attendance or other mandated administrative activities, led to unwillingness to explore the potential in technology for learning and teaching. Risk aversion and a reported lack of strategic leadership resulted in innovation being perceived as individualized. FELTAG also noted that key influencers such as OFSTED and awarding bodies failed to give credit and recognition on what was 'good' or 'outstanding' practice. Tellingly, a London Knowledge Lab (2013: 22) report found a distinct lack of enthusiasm for technology among senior managers due to their '"hand-to-mouth" environment'. FELTAG's recommendations are therefore potentially transformational if they continue to receive ministerial support.

As a practitioner who has been engaged in confidence- and capacity-building activities with students and peers for ten years, it is exciting to be offered an educational vision of the future that recognizes the need for a radical shift to collaborative bottom-up responsibility for innovation; a vision that challenges actions of some senior managers. The cultural shift required is, however, significant and innovators in risk-averse institutions may find themselves further marginalized. FELTAG views initial teacher education (ITE) and CPD as crucial to the sectoral shift, and significantly makes the following recommendations:

> OFSTED's inspection framework to include a requirement for all providers to explicitly embed learning technology in their teaching and learning strategy. OFSTED to increase understanding of quality and effectiveness of technology deployed by providers. Comprehensive training to be provided to OFSTED inspectors to allow them to identify good practice and evaluate the effectiveness of deployed learning technology.

> OFSTED to include a new judgement, 'Capacity to Innovate using learning technology' or include this under Leadership and Management in the Common Inspection Framework.
>
> (FELTAG, 2014: 22)

The seismic shift suggested will require substantial investment as well as a challenge to current norms of accountability and audit. It will be intriguing to observe if FELTAG's courageous 'bungee jumping' (in Barnett's terms) will be implemented. A potential indication of the preparedness of the sector to embrace such risk taking is the publication of the ETF's *Professional Standards for Teachers and Trainers in Education and Training* in May 2014. The Professional Standards Initial Guidance documents states that 'the values and attributes described in the Professional Standards are not "nice to haves"… they are fundamental, integral and essential' and that 'good teachers and trainers … are not afraid to admit developmental needs … including technology knowledge and skills' (2014: 7). The guidance in the appendix suggests how technology might improve students' chances of reaching their potential but this aspiration is unlikely to be achieved without considerable resourcing and cultural change.

The appendix to the Standards also addresses the need for practitioners to be constantly up to date, but worryingly, in light of FELTAG's findings, the first example given of the benefits of technology is using data to track learner progress to plan teaching and cater for individual needs. This activity straddles regulatory and pedagogic domains but it could be argued that such data collection is for institutional audit activity rather than for the teacher and student. That said, in my own practice I do use blogs to track progress and plan for individual needs. My concern here is that the term data is being interpreted in a narrow quantitative rather than in a dialogic sense.

## What has all this got to do with dancing and frivolity?

In this section I offer a reading of the potential for critical and reflective teaching and learning enhanced by the use of technology against the policy backdrop outlined above. My work is guided by a theoretical lens that Shore and Butler (2012: 205) describe as pedagogic gymnastics, bending, juggling and balancing the demands of teaching, management and research in a post-92 university. Barnett's work allows us to view these gymnastics, or pedagogic bungee jumping as he calls it, as a risky but liberational leap into the unknown. Reassuringly he adds: 'there is bound to be uncertainty. A pedagogy of air (as I shall term it) opens up spaces and calls for a will to learn … to learn even amid uncertainty. In the process, it is just possible that the student/teacher may come into another mode of being' (Barnett, 2007: 1). The narratives drawn upon in this section come from ten years of research and dialogue with student teachers undertaking ITE, teacher educators engaging with technology, and qualified teachers undertaking CPD. All of the engagement occurred within a context where embedding technology in ITE was not required and the FE workforce received little systematic support to develop their use of technology.

The technological platform used is not an issue for this chapter. The development of collaborative, dialogic communities supported by technology assists the development of critically reflective practice, which in turn enables negotiation of the risks. In this new landscape 'learning is viewed as a process of participation in a variety of social worlds, and the learner is seen as someone being transformed' (Coffield, 2008: 9). Specifically, the process of becoming a teacher and the sharing of the stories from practice can be supported by an online space that offers the opportunity to safely take risks. M outlines how his leap into the unknown during his ITE did offer a 'new mode of being' (Barnett, 2007: 2), as well as providing a source of sustenance as a new teacher, 'but share I did, making a dreadfully painful experience into something which changed me and maybe others. My shared reflective journal was such a rewarding experience for me personally; I grew in confidence and as a practitioner.'

Chase suggests that writing as a method of inquiry is 'shaped in part by interaction with the audiences' (2005: 656–7). In other words, a narrative is a joint production of narrator and listener. The telling and reshaping of professional identities undertaken by these new teachers through their interactions with peers supports Richardson and Pierre's (2005: 962–6) claim that, 'There is no such thing as "getting it right," only "getting it" differently contoured and nuanced.' E comments:

> The blog … allowed us the safe space to share thoughts, feelings, anxieties, laughter and tears and because it was a shared space we could see the value in the perception of thoughts and opinions of others in the group … The ongoing dialogue with my peers and tutor was fundamental in my development as a reflective writer and new teacher. It was a creative collaborative learning space, a lifeline on what could sometimes be a bumpy road.

Unlike the schools sector there is no Newly Qualified Teacher (NQT) probationary year for FE teachers, so examining the role that technology might play in supporting teachers in their early years of practice is especially apt. E's blog continued to be a lifeline for her group for 18 months following their programme of study.

M also experienced the potential for peer learning as she identified:

> I think what I've noticed most is that they sort of carry on without us more if you know what I mean – whereas traditional teaching and learning is very much teacher at the centre, all information coming out through me but what often is seen to happen ... is that they can talk to each other, they answer each other's questions, they take threads of each other's arguments – really oblivious to the fact that I might be there or might not be there.

This may read as what Barnett identifies as 'pedagogic reciprocity' in that 'teachers and the taught teach each other. Their roles are interwoven, such that their boundaries become indistinct to some extent' (Barnett, 2007: 132). Barnett identifies this as a pedagogy of risk. Barnett's claim that 'pedagogical bungee jumping may be catching' (2007: 133) is illustrated by B's recognition that teaching and learning in this way requires reciprocity and trust:

> It's more holistic, they see the links between the different modules, they see that how they are developing in one area can totally impact on something else, they get to see the growth that's taken place – it's almost like watching themselves from afar because they can see how they worded things, see the language they used, how they interacted, also later on when they need to think about it in their professional capacity they can see that their thought processes have changed as well.

M and B's experiences of collaborative and reciprocal learning cultures reflect Mayes and de Freitas (2007: 13) claim that, 'we are witnessing a new model of education rather than a new model of learning'. Moreover, the examples reflect Gauntlett's analogy of the expansion in internet use in recent decades:

> Websites tended to be like separate gardens ... Web 2.0 describes a particular kind of ethos and approach ... like a collective allotment. Instead of individuals tending their own gardens, they come together to work collaboratively in a shared space.
>
> (Gauntlett, 2011: 5)

A was introduced to this dialogic, reciprocal approach during her early years of practice. As an unqualified teacher she had not experienced this more democratic approach:

> My teaching has completely and utterly changed, totally from how I was taught on the Cert. Ed. – paper based ... sometimes I walk in and there's just images on the screen (on the blog) and that is the teaching and learning of the day. Students don't cope well now with other formats, 'we were talked at for an hour and a half – we go off and do our own learning or you talk to us in a different way.' My teaching has completely altered in just a very short space of time.

A's comment that her students are noticing that the dialogue with others is different and their ability to articulate their own abilities to self-manage gave A the confidence to continue with the frivolous activity. She goes on to say:

> Teaching is very, very different because it's not the detached model. It impacts on how you write your curriculum; it's about empowering the students to be part of the scheme of work. They think I will have ownership of my learning but if I do get stuck there's the blog, there's that scaffolding – it's not just me (tutor), it's all the other peers in there.

Shore and Butler (2012), drawing on Haraway, give the metaphor of the game of cat's cradle to represent the refiguration of learning and teaching that involves the passing of string between multiple players. The constant creation and recreation of the patterns allows A to democratize the learning experience, which includes all of the students in their face-to-face and virtual classrooms. She notes, however, that some of her colleagues hold very different views about the teacher role and the impact of technology on teacher identity and practices:

> Barriers – some teachers are detached, they want to walk out of the door at four o'clock. I think you've got to change, education is changing, you have to change as a teacher and take this technology on and use it.

These practices are causing her to become isolated, as her colleagues don't like how she is blending the teaching and learning. A does not see herself as an expert but she acknowledges that she may be presenting 'an ethical, critical and practical response', in Maclure's (2005) terms, that does not fit with others' educational paradigms:

> It's the fact that other people don't like it enough at the moment. It's the comments I get, it's ok for you, you're IT literate but it's only been two years since I did my IT Level 2. It was facing my fears and addressing them, and other people have to do so.

Despite her isolation A was utterly convinced by this collaborative, dialogue-based approach, which is redolent of the wiliness and persistence of the soldier who adopts the cloak of invisibility in 'The Twelve Dancing Princesses'. Many of the teachers interviewed during the past ten years operated in a culture of invisibility or 'below the wire' activity in their use of technology, as there was no strategic lead and little support from peers. This gap allowed for playful participation and exploration, which underlines Maclure's (2005: 2) suggestion that frivolity may be perceived as resistance.

The fallout from the FELTAG recommendations may have unintended consequences for those teachers who have enjoyed both the dance and the invisibility to date. The playful risks taken by the teachers demonstrate Barnett's (2007: 29) claim that 'the pedagogical being is fragile ... it is brittle, liable to shatter suddenly'. However, B's advice to her risk-averse colleagues demands a more certain leap:

> Get over yourself and do it – you just need to be thrown in at the deep-end and give it a go, and I think that most people would be very surprised by how much it benefits them and although it is slightly more time-consuming at the beginning, eventually it becomes part of your everyday practice.

FELTAG's advice on developing the use of technology in the lifelong learning sector may reflect Barnett's hope for pedagogic reciprocity. The teachers referred to in this chapter express the 'will to live in creative spaces' and they hold the courage to explore 'their associated temporal rhythms' (Barnett, 2010: 81) despite inhibiting cultures. Let's hope that their playful dance thrives, as online learning in the sector develops.

## References

Barnett, R. (2007) *A Will to Learn: Being a student in an age of uncertainty.* Maidenhead: Open University Press.

— (2010) *Being a University.* London: Routledge.

Bolton, G. (2001) *Reflective Practice: Writing and professional development.* London: Paul Chapman.

Chase, S.E. (2005) 'Narrative inquiry: multiple lenses, approaches, voices'. In Denzin, N.K., and Lincoln, Y.S. (eds) *Handbook of Qualitative Research.* Thousand Oaks, CA: Sage.

Coffield, F. (2008) *Just Suppose Teaching and Learning Became the First Priority…* London: LSN.

de Freitas, S., and Jameson, J. (eds) (2012) *The e-Learning Reader*. London: Continuum.

ETF (2014) *Professional Standards for Teachers and Trainers in Education and Training: England*. Online. http://tinyurl.com/qg7fomo (accessed 1 May 2014).

Facer, K. (2011) *Learning Futures: Education, technology and social change*. London: Routledge.

FELTAG (2014) *Further Education Learning Technology Action Group: Recommendations*. Online. http://feltag.org.uk/wp-content/uploads/2012/01/FELTAG-REPORT-FINAL.pdf (accessed 1 April 2015).

Garrison, R., and Anderson, T. (2003) *E-learning in the 21st Century: A framework for research and practice*. London: Routledge.

Gauntlett, D. (2011) *Making is Connecting: The social meaning of creativity, from DIY and knitting to YouTube and Web 2.0*. Cambridge: Polity Press.

Laurillard, D. (2013) *Technology as a driver and enabler of adult vocational teaching and learning*. Online. http://tinyurl.com/qh3lkno (accessed 1 March 2014).

London Knowledge Lab (2013) *The Potential to Coordinate Digital Simulations for UK-wide VET: Report to the commission on adult vocational teaching and learning*. Online. http://tinyurl.com/q448qgz (accessed 31 January 2014).

Luke, D. (1982) *Selected Tales: Jacob and Wilhelm Grimm*. Harmondsworth: Penguin Classics.

Maclure, M. (2005) 'Entertaining doubts: on frivolity as resistance'. Paper presented at Discourse, Power and Resistance Conference, Plymouth, March.

Mayes, T., and de Freitas, S. (2007) 'Learning and e-learning: The role of theory'. In Beetham, H., and Sharpe, R. (eds) *Rethinking Pedagogy for a Digital Age: Designing and delivering e-learning*. London: Routledge, 13–25.

Richardson, L., and St. Pierre, E.A. (2005) 'Writing: A method of inquiry'. In Denzin, N.K., and Lincoln, Y.S. (eds) *The Sage Handbook of Qualitative Research*. 3rd ed. Thousand Oaks, CA: Sage.

Shore, S., and Butler, E. (2012) 'Missing things and methodological swerves: Unsettling the it-ness of VET'. *International Journal of Training Research*, 10 (3), 204–18.

Whitehead, N. (2013) *United Kingdom Commission for Employment and Skills review of adult vocational qualifications* (the Whitehead review). London: UKCES.

'FE was the beginning of my vocational pursuit for a career in dance. It was a time of opportunity, self-discovery, building confidence and empowerment. The staff in the department provided the encouragement and support to ensure that I continued my education and training in HE. We worked together to break down barriers. It was a unique experience.'

Lauren Tucker

# Chapter 5

# Spaces to dance: Community education
## *Jane Weatherby and Lou Mycroft*

*'There was still no likelihood that we could make a living from dance.
We were doing it because we loved it ... We realized how full we felt;
we were surrounded by music and dancing and joy.'*

(Alvin Ailey)

'Once upon a time' is how so many stories begin. And this is no different.
Once upon a time, not so long ago, a sweet seed of an idea was planted,
took root, grew and blossomed ... and we were privileged to help in the
growing of it. Our story is one of community, collectivism, sustainability
and hope. The roots of our current work were put down long ago, in short-
term projects and programmes with the ambitious aim of transforming
communities. The things we learned formed the building blocks of our work
today, as teacher educators. It's been a long journey, and one not without
struggle.

So, here we are, both at home one Sunday morning, 15 years on and
40 miles apart. We're typing into a shared online space and realizing that
the dialogue we are having is more interesting than the traditional narrative
we are supposed to be writing. Join us, if you will, as we chat about what
inspired us to find spaces to dance.

*Jane:* Let's start with 'The Twelve Dancing Princesses' story. How
does that link with your ideas about our work?

*Lou:* In the story, the princesses are kept in a tower by the
tyrannical king, but they escape each night to go dancing; their
shoes are always in tatters by the morning. I think of us sneaking
out the back door of further education, to do work that was
not quite like other people's work, was exhausting and often
misunderstood, but which was both thrilling and transformational
for everyone involved.

*Jane:* I like that, the idea of finding freedom within the constraints
of an institution, looking for ways to push the boundaries, to
be creative in ways that most benefit our students and their
communities. Looking for spaces to dance, without going under

with the stress of all that subversion. Shall we jump straight in and write about the Dealing with Conflict course?

*Lou:* Yes, because that was a massive turning point for us. We were commissioned to do it in the aftermath of the London bombs, because of the fear that growing tensions would fracture local communities.

*Jane:* I remember most that I felt conflicted about doing it and out of my depth. I asked myself how, as a white person, I could possibly stand up and do anti-racist training – but then I thought, if I don't, it's like saying that it's the job of black people to fight racism, and that can't be right, because it's white people who are racist. I also realized that my risk of embarrassment was nothing compared to the oppression black people face every day. What are your memories?

*Lou:* I remember being so fired up to do the work that I had no reservations – and at the same time feeling completely terrified. I had a sense of righting a wrong – I was so angry with the way people seemed to have taken permission from the London bombings to become more openly racist, I wanted to steam in there and put it right. What we'd been doing with the Community Regen programme had become quite safe and familiar and I felt on top of my game. But this was something else.

*Jane:* The Dealing with Conflict programme was about providing community workers with skills and activities they could use to explore issues around race and ethnicity; the groups were really diverse, compared to what we were used to. Looking back, I'm aware of how focused we were on activities, rather than giving people room to talk and reflect – maybe that was out of fear about what might emerge and not being able to contain it.

*Lou:* Yes, thinking about the way we work now, that's the real difference. Now it's all about talking and reflecting; the 'stuff' can be found online. That project was the point at which we started talking openly about our values. You and I reacted differently – we always do. You knew that your integrity was not happy and I was trying not to listen to mine. But our teaching changed during that time because the students' experience was so often humbling. Do you remember the woman in the hijab?

*Jane:* She was sweet, and a bit shy and quietly spoken. She said that since the bombings, she had become wary of going out because of the way people looked at her, because of the way she felt the wearing of the hijab had become linked in people's minds with the word terrorist. I was struck not just by the awfulness of what she described, nor by the crassness of ideas that equated Muslim with terrorist, but also by the way she told this without drama: as just a further twist in her everyday experience. It shook me. You were using non-violent communication (NVC) on that course, weren't you?

*Lou:* Yes and I ended up doing it for real. One of the delegates approached me and asked, 'What right have you, as white trainers, to do anti-racism work?' which had been exactly your reservation with the programme. Her tone was curious, rather than confrontational, and something about it cut through my defensiveness. I can remember the voice in my head saying, 'See! She's found you out!' but kept hold of my wits for long enough to ask her for a little time to think through my response. That afternoon I used NVC live, in front of the group, to figure out my answer.

*Jane:* You were really brave to do that. Is this where we first articulated the connection between values and practice? Now we talk values with students all the time, where before we'd have been pushing them through a sequence of activities. Can you explain a bit more about NVC and say how it related to what we have come to call our 'values work'?

*Lou:* NVC is a conflict resolution process. Essentially, it's a sentence structure that connects how you are feeling in the moment ('angry') with the personal value that is not being nurtured ('honesty'). What NVC did for us was to bring the language of values into our discourse. We began to connect those big value words with the practice principles we held dear, like remembering everyone's name. It made the big stuff doable, somehow, and helped us understand why we did what we did.

*Jane:* I remember reading Michael Newman about that time, who says it's not possible to be neutral, to be neutral is to side with the powerful. That made such an impact, because there was still an idea in me that we were facilitators rather than teachers, that we shouldn't 'impose' our ideas on learners. The notion that our values inevitably linked to our practice, and that we needed to honestly and explicitly acknowledge this, grew in strength the more we thought about it.

*Lou:* It was a fundamental change. Do you remember the Learning for Democracy stuff? We discovered that around the same time and it also challenged received thinking around educator 'neutrality'. Talking values and practice principles led us to explore teacher identity and impostor syndrome too, and the denial implicit in that. I think from that point, we were always going to move into teacher education.

*Jane:* I'm thinking now about the way we drew inspiration from other people's ideas, and how these have helped sustain us. I love that moment when you are reading something and it resonates absolutely with your own experience, or else it answers a question that you didn't even know you had. You introduced this idea to the students really well, by using one of their comments: 'Thinkers are our friends.' I love this, because I do think of them in this way, as people I go to for a chat when I'm struggling with something. We always refer to them by their first names now. Who have been your most influential friends?

*Lou:* You know who I'm going to say, don't you? It's Nancy, for me. Nancy Kline. I was defensive about Nancy for a long time, because she didn't seem 'academic'. I had impostor syndrome on her behalf! But those days are long gone. My teaching is so profoundly influenced by her concept of the Thinking Environment that I can't see the join; being a Thinking Environment practitioner has become part of my teaching identity. And I see the impact of those simple rules: if you create conditions where people will listen to one another, that collective attention will generate the finest critical thinking, again and again. Who are your thinking friends?

*Jane:* As well as Michael Newman, I'd have to say Stephen Brookfield. I never read Stephen without learning something new, and I go back to books that are now more than 15 years old and they still talk to me. I love the way he encourages you to confront your own assumptions, and to think honestly about teaching and learning, to acknowledge that it's hard and messy. It was Stephen, too, who made me first think more critically and reflexively, to recognize that our work is shaped by ideologies and that we need to question why we do as we do, and to consider more than our personal perspective.

*Lou:* bell hooks was a slow burn for me, you had been influenced by her a long time before but I was still at the stage of dismantling denial about the privileges I had, and felt she was shouting at me. My students inspired me to pick her up again the other year and this time I got it – she was shouting *for* me. I love her passionate hopefulness and the way in which she challenges us not to stand by.

*Jane:* bell *is* quite shouty, but I love her for that, and for the love in her writing. She's brave and challenging and difficult. She's the embodiment for me of someone who is clear about her values and how they underpin her practice as a teacher. She comes under enormous pressure to conform by the institutions in which she works, yet she fights this. She looks for places to dance, if you like. We haven't mentioned Paulo yet. bell is a big fan, and her writings about him made me appreciate him even more.

*Lou:* Paulo Freire is all the way through this, isn't he? Even the word 'animateur', the name of the first project that brought us together, has its roots in Paulo somewhere. We came late to him in a sense and there was already a backlash about some of his ideas, but bell faced that head on, didn't she?

*Jane:* The story about how she challenges him in front of her whole faculty is really moving. She expects him to be angry when she asks why his work ignores the oppression of women, but he doesn't respond with anger, he says she's right, and that he recognizes this was a mistake, and bell says that this is the moment she knows she loves him. More recently I've enjoyed Stephen Kemmis' ideas, too. He sets out a way of thinking, about the impact of learning on individuals and the wider community, which struck such a chord, because we've always striven to grasp that balance. I really like his definition of praxis too. It links together action, history-making and moral good.

*Lou:* David Price's book *Open* has helped me make sense of the way social media has transformed the way we work. That feeling of being part of an open movement across leadership, education and journalism; it's democratizing, world-changing stuff. Etienne Wenger and Jean Lave were visionaries all those years ago, before the technology was there to fully illuminate what a community of practice could be.

*Jane:* There's a common thread in all of these that links to the Learning for Democracy principles. All these thinkers and their ideas have given us strength. The other major impact has been technology. It's made dialogue and the exploration of ideas so much more fluid; the fact that we have platforms that intersect but are different. Spaces to investigate our thoughts and values, to work reflexively. That brings a sense of satisfaction and purposefulness, which are sustaining, especially when we've felt at risk of being locked up in the tower again.

*Lou:* Yes, to pose questions, post material, challenge and be challenged, to drink from the well of support. And to lurk.

*Jane:* I really appreciate the notion of lurking and listening as being valid forms of participation. There is room to tease out ideas in a way that face-to-face discussions don't always allow. You are sometimes constrained by not wanting to take up too much of someone's time, or by not being able to verbally articulate your thoughts clearly. But the variety of platforms within what we now call the Community of Praxis work really well to enable this. We should explain what this is.

*Lou:* The Community of Praxis is what we call the network of students, tutors, graduates and critical friends, who gather in both social media and face-to-face spaces, to talk social-purpose education. The actual spaces develop and change over time, both technically and in terms of the 'personality' of the space.

It's exactly what we needed back in the days of the Community Regen programme, but we didn't know it then. We encountered some passionate, dominant people: people who had been unsung, unthanked and unnoticed. No wonder that some of them, having finally found a voice, didn't want to stop talking. But there was so little space for the quieter members of the group to dance. Like the princesses, we had a peek through the trapdoor at a new online world but the technology hadn't quite caught up with us. Social media was clunky 15 years ago and it took too much energy on our part to sustain.

*Jane:* I'm going to say honestly that I was resistant when the most recent forays into online dialogue began, because the only platform that we had, which worked, was Facebook. There were lots of reasons for using it, because it was part of students' lives already. But I didn't like what Facebook represents, and I was uncomfortable with the blurring of people's personal lives and their personas as teachers and learners. Profile pictures, for example, were sometimes incongruent with teaching roles. I was also conscious that some people were excluded because they didn't use it. As more technology has evolved, I feel less worried. It's more familiar, there is more of a choice, and as people have become aware of their online identities, they are more thoughtful about what and where they post.

*Lou:* I've had so much stick over Facebook! Out of all the freely available platforms, it's the one that most provokes polarized thinking, to the point of rudeness at times. Now there's a choice of platforms, people go where they feel most comfortable, to listen or to speak. Some will always favour face-to-face interaction, but most people, it seems, like a bit of both, which is great affirmation of our blended approach. It seems to me that the Community of Praxis is what was missing from our work in those early days, the equalizing, democratizing force. What do you think?

*Jane:* I can see the seeds of it in the strength of the team we worked within, and the support we gave each other which helped sustain us and our work. But you are right. Some voices were louder than others, and our team didn't include any students. What's so good now is that as teacher educators our students are also colleagues. I have a genuine sense of that, not because they work in the same institution – they don't – but because the Community of Praxis has created an environment to talk about issues, some relatively frivolous, but some really serious and fundamental principles. I have learned so much, both from people's contributions, but also from reflecting on my own responses to them.

*Lou:* This is a book for educators who haven't become cynical. Has the Community of Praxis rescued us from that fate?

*Jane:* I always used to feel that you had to grow cynical and then grow out of it in order to survive. That was in any case true for me. What the Community of Praxis has done is to re-energize my thinking about education. I really appreciate the way I can leave a comment about a philosophical struggle I might be having on Facebook, and come back a few days later to read responses. It's interesting the way the platforms work together too. Yammer gets used a lot for practical discussions but people also post there about their dilemmas. The blogs have allowed people to write freely in any way they want. I don't use Twitter much, but I really like the way you can just re-Tweet a link to a thought-provoking article, or distil some complex idea into a short sentence. The face-to-face contact does, of course, make an impact on how much people interact, but I'm also struck by how much people from across different spheres engage with one another.

*Lou:* The platforms themselves, and I include the face-to-face spaces, are diverse. There's something totalitarian about the princesses' tale, something identikit in the way that they all put their shoes on and go to meet the princes. What the Community of Praxis has given us is the space to go off and dance where and how we want, dance with freedom to be present as ourselves. We don't have to be alone because we can tag people in, or they come and join us anyway. This is where rhizomatic learning comes into it for me. Should we say a bit about what that is?

*Jane:* When I see the word rhizome I think about Jerusalem artichokes, which makes me think about gardening, and all the gardening I am not doing at the moment, and what my plans for my garden are and should be. That thread of thinking sort of embodies the concept for me. It's an idea that turns the community into the curriculum, so what is taught and learned is framed by the dialogue that happens. There is no session plan or PowerPoint to follow. People make connections between sometimes seemingly disparate ideas, and this process, like a rhizome that spreads underground, throws up new shoots of learning.

*Lou:* Rhizomatic learning has really taken us back to the earliest days of our work, even before we wrote units of accreditation, when we used to rock up together with the students and say, 'What do you want to do today?' At the same time, the difference between then and now is fundamentally immense. Then, we were naive enough to believe that just asking the question was empowerment enough. No wonder some people opted out of the blank page we essentially offered them. Now, we understand that it takes a lot of getting to the point where anyone can truly think for themselves – us too.

*Jane:* Yes, because previously we were constrained by the discourses around us, about what teaching and learning *is*: for example the idea that if someone doesn't speak in class that must mean they're not learning anything. We discussed this the other night in the Community of Praxis.

*Lou:* Back to the lurkers. We wrote a blog post in honour of lurkers after a few people used the word to describe themselves and it was wonderful to see how many hitherto unheard voices popped up – 'I'm a lurker! Is it really OK?'

*Jane:* I think this illustrates the way the Community of Praxis works. Lurking emerged as a theme and moved onto discussions about students not speaking in class, and our frustration as teachers and learners ourselves with the instrumental way participation is taken to mean speaking by current observation practice. People shared examples of their own experiences and we concluded that lurking was not just OK, but valid.

*Lou:* Being yourself is OK in the Community of Praxis, we've observed (and felt) that and we've also learned that, in true Open Space tradition, the people there are the right people. We do take care in the formal part of the programme (the courses) to ensure that ground rules are negotiated to cover online engagement, as well as face-to-face. But many of the people who join the online spaces don't visit our college, don't live in the UK, even, and they are still very much part of the community that shapes the social-purpose education curriculum. What makes the Community of Praxis such a safe space to be yourself?

*Jane:* It's a safe space for me because I believe in the value base, values that are around democracy, equality, diversity and a desire to act upon the world to change it for the better. These play out explicitly in the content of the discussions that we have, but also in the way they are conducted. There's a culture of respect that has its roots in the work of Nancy [Kline], I think. No one gets shouted down, and so people are courageous in acknowledging their uncertainties. A recent dialogue about what is your authentic voice, and who gets to judge, was fascinating, and freed me up to be less precious and fearful about putting my words out there for people to read.

Now, I think we need to try to draw this together. I'm very conscious that what has worked for us and helped us to maintain the spaces to dance in our own way, may not translate to other contexts. What points and principles do you think are the most important? What messages do you want people to take away with them?

*Lou:* Keep finding spaces to dance. A decade ago, we had an OFSTED Inspector cornered in a classroom by students who were frustrated that he couldn't see how their learning impacted on community empowerment. Last time we were inspected, our social-purpose philosophy was totally affirmed. The world changes and new spaces open up. Also I want to say that I could not have done this on my own. That's why it's a 'Princesses' story and not a 'Red Riding Hood' one with its lone wolf metaphor. All the fresh and energetic thinking that has got us to this point simply could not happen in one person's head. That the 'team' now includes students, graduates and people we've never met, all operating in a Thinking Environment, makes it liberating. 'Education as the Practice of Freedom.' What's your stand-out message?

*Jane:* I've just read yours, and I can think of no better person to end with than bell [hooks], thank you. She's bolshy, and fierce, and loving, and gentle, and she pushes me out of my comfort zone to make me confront things I would otherwise complacently overlook. She's helped make me braver when I lacked courage.

And of course, that's what the Community of Praxis has also done. Even before we named it, the support we drew from each other, from colleagues we've had and lost, from students whose names have sometimes faded from memory. My message is to not give up on looking for space to dance, because it's still there.

We begin and end with collectivism. We may need to separate and retrace our own steps from time to time, but in the end, the way we dance together – all together, now – is the stuff of transformation, and of hope.

## Further reading

Albee, A., and Boyd, G. (1997) *Doing it Differently: Networks of community development agents*. Edinburgh: Scottish Community Education Council.

Brookfield, S.D. (1995) *Becoming a Critically Reflective Teacher*. San Francisco: Jossey-Bass.

Cormier, D. (2011) *Rhizomatic Learning: Why we teach? Dave's Educational Blog*. Online. http://tinyurl.com/d525eqc (accessed 20 March 2014).

Freire, P. (1996) *Pedagogy of the Oppressed*. London: Penguin.

hooks, b. (1994) *Teaching to Transgress: Education as the practice of freedom*. London: Routledge.

— (2003) *Teaching Community: A pedagogy of hope*. London: Routledge.

Hope, A., and Timmel, S. (1996) *Training for Transformation: A handbook for community workers*. Rugby: Practical Action Publishing.

Kemmis, S., Wilkinson, J., Edwards-Groves, C., Hardy, I., Grootenboer, P., and Bristol, L. (2014) *Changing Practice, Changing Education*. London: Springer.

Kline, N. (2009) *More Time to Think*. Pool-in-Wharfedale: Fisher King.

Lave, J., and Wenger, E. (1991) *Situated Learning: Legitimate peripheral participation*. Cambridge: Cambridge University Press.

Learning for Democracy Group (2008) *Ten Propositions and Ten Proposals*. Online. http://tinyurl.com/ohckueh (accessed 1 March 2014).

Newman, M. (2006) 'Throwing out the balance with the bathwater'. *The encyclopaedia of informal education*. Online. http://tinyurl.com/p86magf (accessed 1 June 2014).

— (2006) *Teaching Defiance: Stories and strategies for activist educators*. San Francisco: Jossey-Bass.

Owen, H. (2008) *Open Space Technology: A user's guide*. 3rd ed. Oakland, CA: Berrett-Koehler.

Price, D. (2013) *Open: How we'll work, live and learn in the future*. London: Crux.

Rosenberg, M.B. (2006) *Non-violent Communication: A language for life*. Encinitas, CA: PuddleDancer Press.

'FE gave me the knowledge, the confidence and the sincere belief that I could become successful in my subject. It gave me the tools and more to progress to HE and work in a profession that I am so passionate about.'

Nicola Rea Davis

# Breaking free from the regulation of the state: The pursuit to reclaim lesson observation as a tool for professional learning in FE
*Matt O'Leary*

> '*Dance as though no one is watching you.*'
>
> (Attributed to Alfred D. Souza)

## Introduction

Government policy in the FE sector in England has focused heavily on improving the quality of teaching in recent years, with lesson observation playing an increasingly important role. Yet, as with the plight of the twelve dancing princesses, the way in which teachers have experienced observation has been predominantly controlled by the narrative of a strong sovereign power, in this case, the state regulator OFSTED. To date, current practice has been principally concerned with attempting to measure teacher performance for accountability and benchmarking purposes rather than actually improving it. This has led to the hegemony of lesson observation as a performative tool of managerialist systems and its subsequent dilution as a catalyst for professional learning. Just as the princesses in the Brothers Grimm tale were made to feel like prisoners in their own home by their controlling father, so too have practitioners come to experience increased levels of disempowerment, anxiety and general discontent in relation to the use of observation in the workplace. In drawing on data from recent research carried out in the FE sector, this chapter examines the context surrounding the hegemony of performative observation, along with evidence of an emerging culture of counter-hegemony and subversion by those who are committed to prioritizing the development needs of their colleagues ahead of the demands of data-led surveillance systems. These counter-hegemonic practices can be seen to offer opportunities for institutions and individuals alike to reclaim observation as a tool for empowering professional learning and in so doing bring about a richer understanding of teaching and learning, and ultimately the much sought-after improvement in standards.

Lesson observation has an established role in the education, training and continuing professional development (CPD) of teachers in the English education system. It has traditionally served a dual purpose. On the one hand it is a method for assessing teacher competence and performance, and on the other it is a stimulus for fostering key pedagogic skills and teacher learning. Over the years, observation has thus come to be connected largely with the domains of initial teacher education (ITE) and teacher appraisal, in one form or another. In spite of this longstanding history, it is only over the last two decades that practitioners in colleges and schools in England have witnessed the widespread use of lesson observations, as governmental agencies such as OFSTED and employers have come to depend on them for collecting evidence about the quality of educational provision. Such evidence has typically formed the basis of judgements about the performance and competence of teachers, along with informing the debate on what makes for effective teaching and learning. Thus, in short, lesson observation has rapidly become a vital mechanism of performance management systems for teaching and learning in colleges and schools across England (O'Leary, 2012).

In focusing specifically on the FE context, this chapter discusses the use and impact of lesson observation on the professional lives of practitioners. It draws on aspects of critical theory, notably Gramsci's (1971) concepts of hegemony and counter-hegemony and Foucault's (1977) concept of normalization, to make sense of some of the wider issues that underpin discussions about how teachers experience observation. This can be linked to the predicament of the twelve dancing princesses. These are issues of power, control, trust and freedom.

The chapter begins with a brief policy backdrop to lesson observation in the FE sector and seeks to outline how and why observation has become one of the most important means of collecting evidence about the quality of teaching and learning in recent years. Drawing on findings from recent research into the use of observation in FE, the chapter then examines the contexts and cultures surrounding the hegemony of performance-driven models of observation. It introduces evidence of an emerging culture of counter-hegemony in some institutions. It argues that in these counter-hegemonic spaces practitioners are most likely to experience the kind of freedom enjoyed by the princesses who escape the confines of the king's castle each night. Furthermore, in such spaces the greatest gains are likely to be made in improving teaching and the student experience.

## Contextualizing lesson observation in FE: the policy backdrop

The chapter cannot provide an in-depth account of the context and rationale for the emergence of observation, as this requires piecing together myriad education policies and initiatives produced as part of the ongoing reform agenda in FE. Besides, this has been discussed at length elsewhere (see Chapter 2 in O'Leary, 2014). However, it is worth making the point that many of these policies and initiatives were initially, and continue to be, driven by a neoliberal agenda intent on pursuing public-sector improvement through an unyielding reliance on managerialist systems. The FE sector, in particular, has a history as a testing ground for public-policy reforms. The political agenda of successive governments has been to open up educational provision to the forces of marketization and the accompanying technologies of managerialism and performativity. These have become ubiquitous terms in the literature and in studies of how FE providers have operated since the early 1990s. These terms had a role in the emergence of lesson observation in FE, first under the New Labour administration (1997–2010) and then the Conservative–Liberal Democrat Coalition Government of 2010–15.

Following a landslide victory in 1997, New Labour wasted no time in implementing the education reform agenda that had been a key driver in its election manifesto. The relentless speed with which policies were introduced was indicative of how highly education reform ranked among its political priorities and the FE sector experienced a period of constant change during the New Labour administration. It was committed to raising the profile of FE so it would play a key role in raising the skill level of the nation's workforce. But the government realized that, for this to happen, it needed to invest in improving the knowledge and skills base of those teaching in the sector. This in turn led to reforms such as the creation of professional teacher standards and a new set of teaching qualifications, along with a new common inspection framework (CIF) under OFSTED. These reforms were seen as fundamental to developing the FE workforce but also as key to ensuring increased accountability.

Lesson observation emerged as an important means of gathering evidence for FE providers' quality systems and preparing for OFSTED inspections. Over the course of the last decade observation has quickly evolved into a catch-all crucible in which performance data and evidence of improvements in teaching and learning bubble away together. Graded observation, in particular, has come to epitomize Foucault's (1977) notion of the 'examination', where a teacher's performance is categorized and differentiated by the observer according to OFSTED's four-point scale. Arguably, what has led to this reliance on observation as a source of evidence is its convenience as a reductive mechanism used to fulfil multiple purposes and one through which the day-to-day systems of managerialism, such as quality assurance, target setting and continuous improvement, are experienced as a microcosm.

This emphasis on observation intensified further when the Coalition Government took office in May 2010. The focus on teaching and learning as the main vehicle for driving up standards in education and extending the agenda for continuous improvement subsequently entered a new phase of heightened surveillance and accountability. The repercussions have resulted in even higher-stakes assessment of teachers' practice in schools and colleges. In the schools sector, for example, the white paper, *The Importance of Teaching* (Department for Education, 2010), pledged greater use of observation and increased powers for head teachers in schools to 'sit in on as many lessons as necessary to root out under-performing teachers'. Observation is identified as a key tool in the improvement of practice and considered the principal means of reinstating what is regarded as core in education.

Even before the white paper was published, the proposal drew criticism from the main teaching unions who saw it as a management surveillance stick with which to beat teachers. This particular concern has since been heightened following cases in both colleges and schools where teachers have taken industrial action against the imposition of what they have perceived as punitive observation policies imposed on them by senior managers. Often such policies have made direct links between the outcomes of performance management graded observations and formal capability procedures. In other words, they have become a disciplinary mechanism, which has afforded senior management increased control over teachers' practice and even their continued employment. Lesson observation has become, therefore, a highly charged and contested mechanism for many in the teaching profession.

## The hegemony and normalization of graded lesson observations

The concept of hegemony is associated with the Italian Marxist Antonio Gramsci. Underpinning Gramsci's concept of hegemony is an analysis that explains consent in maintaining and supporting existing unequal power relations. People accept the values and practices of those in authority because they are mistakenly perceived as being unassailable common sense and even in their own interests. But what is the relevance of the concept of hegemony to our discussion about the use of lesson observation in FE and how can it help to illuminate our understanding of it? As we shall see when examining findings from recent research, below, the practice of grading lesson observations has become normalized across FE with only very few providers choosing to diverge from the norm. This is, of course, heavily determined by the control of OFSTED. Many providers are reluctant to do anything that might be deemed to contravene OFSTED's favoured practice for fear of drawing unwanted attention to themselves, particularly those awaiting an inspection and/or those not currently adjudged to be 'outstanding' or 'good'. But before we continue this discussion, let us first clarify what 'graded lesson observations' actually are.

Graded observations are summative assessments of a teacher's classroom competence and performance, typically undertaken on an annual basis and culminating in the award of a grade based on OFSTED's CIF four-point scale. These grades are then entered into institutions' quality management systems, where they are used in performance management as well as to provide evidence for inspection purposes. These quantitative performance indicators, or what is commonly referred to in the sector as the 'observation grade profile' (that is, a statistical dataset of how many lessons were graded 1, 2, 3 or 4 in any given year within the institution), have quickly become an established feature of FE performance management systems. Although questions remain about the validity and reliability of such systems, the observation grade profile is commonly cited in the sector. It is used to compare overall performance, year-on-year, forming the basis for a provider's self-assessment for inspection purposes.

In 2013 the main FE teachers' union, the University and College Union, sponsored a national research project into the use and impact of lesson observation in FE (O'Leary, 2013b). In the online survey phase of the data collection, respondents were asked to indicate the context that best described their most recent experience of observation. In total there were 3,958 questionnaires returned, of which 3,525 were fully completed and 432 partially completed. The University and College Union (UCU) FE membership was reported to be approximately 32,000 at the time the survey was circulated, thus there was an overall response rate of just over 11 per cent from the membership.

As Figure 6.1 illustrates, the most common response chosen by over two-thirds (68.6 per cent) was the internal quality assurance (QA) scheme, where the lesson is evaluated and graded against the OFSTED four-point scale. Similarly, the context of 'external consultation' grades observations against the OFSTED scale and is used as a 'Mocksted', where external consultants are employed to carry out observations as though it were part of an inspection. When combined, the first three contexts listed in Figure 6.1, all of which adopted a similar performance management approach, amounted to over four-fifths (84.4 per cent) of responses.

**7. Which of the contexts below best describes your most recent experience of lesson observation in your workplace?**

| | Response Percent | Response Count |
|---|---|---|
| Internal Quality Assurance scheme | 68.6% | 2,704 |
| Ofsted inspection | 6.8% | 268 |
| External consultation/mock inspection | 9.0% | 353 |
| Peer review/peer development | 11.0% | 434 |
| Other (please state) | 4.6% | 181 |
| answered question | | 3,940 |
| skipped question | | 36 |

Figure 6.1: Contexts of lesson observation

Following on from this, responses to the question shown in Figure 6.2 sought to categorize the particular models of observation that were most commonly used in FE. Unsurprisingly, there were correlations between these responses and those discussed in Figure 6.1. Thus, the 'managerial, graded model' accounted for over four-fifths (83.5 per cent) of responses, whereas ungraded models just over a tenth (13.3 per cent).

**8. Which of the models of lesson observation described below is most commonly used in your workplace?**

| | | Response Percent | Response Count |
|---|---|---|---|
| Managerial, graded model using internal observers | | 76.7% | 3,018 |
| Managerial, graded model using external observers | | 6.8% | 267 |
| Developmental, ungraded model with jointly agreed action plan by observer and observee | | 10.0% | 394 |
| Ungraded, peer model without action plan | | 3.3% | 128 |
| Other (please state) | | 3.2% | 127 |
| | answered question | | 3,934 |
| | skipped question | | 42 |

**Figure 6.2:** Models of lesson observation

The fact that lesson observation has become associated with performance management in FE in recent years is a consequence of the wider political and economic 'neoliberal reform agenda' that has sought to 'transform the working cultures of public sector institutions' (O'Leary, 2014: 11). The widespread use of graded observations is thus a predictable consequence of this and, in particular, of the increasing control and influence of OFSTED. Since its involvement in FE, OFSTED's role has moved beyond that of inspecting standards to one of defining them, with the result that certain models of self-assessment have become normalized. This has been the case with graded observations.

Viewed through a Foucauldian lens, the decision of FE providers to embrace the graded observations, which have themselves become hegemonic, is an example of government and aligned agencies like OFSTED casting their 'normalising gaze' over the sector (Foucault, 1977: 184). Just as the twelve dancing princesses' father, the king, sought to exercise control over their lives, so too does the state, under the auspices of OFSTED, control notions of quality in educational provision. While performative exercises such as inspections and internal quality audits represent key components of surveillance, their effects are apparent before and after these activities occur. As Foucault reminds us, 'surveillance is permanent in its effects, even if it is discontinuous in its action' (ibid.: 201). Whether or not the dancing princesses are aware of the presence of the old soldier who acts as an invisible spy and ultimately reveals their secret, what they and teachers have in common is that their actions are subjected to surveillance, which is built on the premise of mistrust.

Underpinning this process of continuous surveillance is the concept of normalization. Foucault maintained that 'the power of normalisation imposes homogeneity' (ibid.). Yet normalization simultaneously individualizes as it encourages the identification of gaps or, in the case of graded observations, instances of assessed performance that in the eyes of the observer do not correspond with hegemonic notions of effective teaching and learning. OFSTED's four-point scale has thus become the instrument of normalizing judgement, which operates as a corrective tool to determine if teachers have reached prescribed standards of practice and to modify behaviour.

This dominance of the performative use of observation has resulted in FE teachers becoming increasingly conditioned to being graded on their classroom performance whenever they are observed, regardless of the context and purpose of the observation. Thus, for some teachers, the process of observation and the act of grading against the OFSTED scale have become inseparable, particularly for those who have only worked in the sector for the last decade and have known nothing else. As Brian, one of the participants in the UCU study, comments:

> We're so used to getting a grade now when we're observed that even if a colleague does something like a peer observation of you, there's a part of you that still wants to know how they'd grade it, even though that's not the point.
>
> (O'Leary, 2013b: 43)

Such engrained perceptions of observation are a consequence of what Foucault (Gordon, 1980) described as the 'apparatuses of control', which create 'dominant discourses' and 'regimes of truth' that establish certain forms of knowledge as more legitimate and valuable than others. As the regulator of standards and quality for the sector, the dominant discourses of OFSTED inevitably play a central role in shaping the way in which FE staff make sense of and interpret the function of observation, as well as defining the parameters within which they are given licence to do so.

Smith and O'Leary (2013) have argued that these 'regimes of truth' have given rise to the domination of what they refer to as 'managerialist positivism' in evaluating educational provision, where the complexity of the teaching and learning process is reduced to the presentation of quantitative performance data, which is valued more highly than qualitative data on the premise that their 'measurability' gives an increased sense of rigour and credibility. They have argued that managerialist positivism 'can be seen as the ideological veil that normalizes the representation of complex sociological and qualitative phenomena in reductive and numerical forms' (ibid.: 246). That practitioners are actively resisting such normalized practice should not be interpreted as a reckless refusal to comply or obey the authority of OFSTED, but a reflection of deeper concerns regarding the legitimacy and reliability of its assessment framework and the impact of that on teachers.

As commented above, the compilation and scrutiny of statistical data from annual graded observations is seen as an essential part of the performance management cycle for senior managers in monitoring and assessing the quality of teaching and learning across the institution. This is despite the scepticism expressed by senior managers such as Graham, who is openly critical of such practice in the following comment:

> At the end of the year in our self-assessment report, we will report on the number of ones, twos, threes and fours and I think it's basically worthless but it's something that all colleges do at the moment because it's what OFSTED expects.
>
> (O'Leary, 2014: 23)

Although it is not explicitly stated anywhere in OFSTED documentation that providers are required to produce the observation grade profile when preparing evidence for inspections, there is, as Graham states, an implicit expectation that such data should be made available. His remark that 'it's what OFSTED expects' would no doubt strike a familiar chord with many senior managers who are reluctant to move away from graded observations for fear of failing to comply with the hegemony of normalized practice. That would make their colleges stand out and potentially leave them more open to the critical scrutiny of OFSTED. In the following quote, Paul, a senior manager from another college, illustrates this by recounting how his college considered changing to an ungraded model of observation but with an OFSTED inspection looming decided not to do so:

> We had links with another outstanding college and knew they'd decided to scrap grading altogether, although they did this shortly after a successful OFSTED inspection and it's quite interesting when you look at the colleges that do abandon grading. They're almost exclusively colleges who have just been through a successful OFSTED inspection so they're not expecting an inspection team to return for a number of years. We weren't in that position because we were inspected in 2009 so we are

expecting to be inspected this year. So we didn't really feel the time was right or it might be advisable to lose grading altogether just before an inspection.

(O'Leary, 2013b: 49)

Not only do Paul's comments reinforce theories of the hegemony and normalization of graded observations in FE, but they also provide an insight into the reluctance of many senior managers to challenge this practice by exploring alternative and/or ungraded models of observation. Many are apprehensive about doing anything that might be looked upon unfavourably by OFSTED or draw unsolicited attention to themselves, particularly those awaiting an inspection. Yet this is in spite of a growing bank of evidence calling into question the fitness for purpose of current normalized models of observation and highlighting their counterproductive consequences (e.g. O'Leary, 2013b). For Paul, those providers recently judged successful were more likely to experiment with counter-hegemonic approaches, as 'they're not expecting an inspection team to return for a number of years', and, as such, were afforded more freedom to do so. However, as the case study of Rainbow College in the following section illustrates, the rationale for exploring alternatives is sometimes driven more by the underlying values and beliefs of senior managers than the outcomes of the last OFSTED inspection.

## Counter-hegemonic practices

The UCU study revealed numerous instances of counter-hegemonic approaches to observation in practice, although many tended to operate on the peripheries of formal systems of accountability. Ungraded models of observation, for example, were in use in some institutions, though only accounted for a tenth of responses (see Figures 6.1 and 6.2 above). Similarly, peer observation, while not uncommon in some workplaces, occurred mainly as an informal, unaccredited activity that staff undertook on a voluntary basis. These alternative models were rarely viewed by senior managers with the same level of importance as their performative counterparts and tended to be valued more highly by practitioners.

Even in those workplaces where professional autonomy was heavily circumscribed, there was still evidence of resistance to the dominant discourses of managerialism and performativity. Like Gramsci's notion of counter-hegemony, Foucault maintained that wherever there are dominant discourses and regimes of truth, 'there are always also movements in the opposite direction' (Gordon, 1980: 199). In a study involving ten colleges in the West Midlands, three managers and observers in particular – Abdul,

Cristina and Molly – embodied this resistance and challenge. Despite having gone through a significant culture change as a result of a merger with another large college that saw the introduction of a punitive observation scheme, they refused to compromise their commitment to putting the professional development needs of their observees at the forefront of their role as observers. In doing so, they were countering the managerialist and performative ideology underpinning the newly formed college's approach, as illustrated in the following comment by Abdul:

> I'm fighting it because regardless of what people above tell me I should be doing and how I should be doing it, I'm still going to be doing the observations in a supportive way. I can write it up in any way they want but I'm still going to carry out the process in a very supportive way and that's what's at the heart of it for me.
>
> (O'Leary, 2013a: 358)

Abdul's emphasis on the 'supportive' element of the observation process was echoed in the accounts of other observers. For instance, Molly talked about occasions where she had decided to 'walk away' from an observation when it was clear that the member of staff was 'having a bad day'. Instead of entering a poor grade for the original observation on that day, she would renegotiate an alternative lesson to observe in order to allow the observee the opportunity to 'demonstrate their real capabilities as a teacher'. Other examples of counter-hegemonic and subversive practice included the negotiation of grades between observer and observee, even though such practices appeared to contravene official observation protocol in those providers.

## The ungraded 'ESCP' model at Rainbow College: a case study

As part of a new institutional policy designed to 'move from teaching to learning', Rainbow College implemented an ungraded model of observation, which they referred to as the ESCP (Engage, Support, Challenge, Progress) model. The ESCP shares similar principles to that of lesson study in terms of putting student and teacher learning at the centre of the observation process rather than teacher evaluation. The following list of bullet points, taken from an internal document of Rainbow College, summarizes the 'key principles' of their ESCP approach:

- focus on engaging, supporting, challenging and progressing all learners
- focus on learning rather than teaching

- focus on a holistic view of the learning experience
- develop learning conversations
- embed quality improvement practice
- focus on joint practice development with all members of the college community learning from each other
- embed observation and visits within general practice rather than as one-off performances
- being a supportive and developmental process, no formal capability process shall be initiated against any staff as a result of this process.

These key principles were to form the foundation for the college's new approach to observation and pave the way for making the transition from the previous system. Penny, the college's Head of Quality, commented that the previous system had focused heavily on assessing and judging individual teacher performance. As a result of feedback from staff focus groups, staff evaluations and discussions with the college's team of observers, the college decided that it was time to review and reform its approach to lesson observation. Penny and her colleagues were determined to act on the feedback from college staff and move towards a new system where the focus would be switched from individual teacher performance to evaluating the learners' experience and exploring the impact of teaching on that experience. In the following interview extract, Penny describes how the ESCP model worked in practice at Rainbow College:

> There are four separate 'events' if you like. There's a pre-observation meeting, observation, traditional feedback and then a follow up, which is kind of time consuming, but what we have said now is that the pre-observation meeting can be by phone if it's too difficult to meet. The feedback might be short and what we do hope is that it's something that's valuable and it's about what we do. I do think we spend too much time doing forms rather than discussions and that's something we wanted to change, you know, put the emphasis on the discussions rather than form filling.

> (O'Leary, 2013b: 83)

In Penny's description of Rainbow's ESCP model, she emphasized the importance of dialogue between observer and observee. This was reflected in the prominent role it played in the different stages of the model, with three of the 'four events' consisting of discussions between observer and observee. What was also noticeable was the inclusion of a pre-observation meeting and a follow-up discussion to the observation feedback. The former is not common practice across the sector, but is considered an important element in making the observation process more collaborative and increasing teacher ownership, as has been commented in recent studies:

> The inclusion of a pre-observation meeting is another important aspect of increasing teacher ownership of the process. With most assessment models of observation, the pre-observation meeting is a rare occurrence. Not only does this provide both observer and observee with an opportunity to discuss the focus of the lesson and for the latter to provide a rationale for their choice, but also enables them to negotiate a set of shared goals that takes into account the needs of the individual and the institution.
>
> (O'Leary, 2014: 120).

This view of the pre-observation meeting was confirmed by Penny in the following description of how she envisaged these meetings:

> They would arrange to meet a teacher before the observation, what we call the pre-observation discussion and talk about the teaching and what the teacher would like them to observe, which is mutually decided and basically it's to be more focused on innovation and development so you would choose to try something out with your observer. You would also identify what particular strand you wanted feedback on, so the teacher being observed plays a key role in deciding the focus of the observation.
>
> (O'Leary, 2013b: 84)

The ESCP model thus appeared to offer a means of framing the discussion between observer and observee, as well as providing them with a set of discourse and phenomena to reflect on and self-evaluate their chosen area(s) of practice. What was also noteworthy of this model was the focus on 'innovation and development', where observees were encouraged to 'try something out'. This willingness to experiment and take risks in one's teaching is considered fundamental to the CPD of tutors (see, for example, Institute for Learning, 2012), yet opportunities to do so often depend upon the extent to which an institution entrusts its staff with the necessary professional autonomy.

In the following extract, Penny uses the metaphor of a multi-layered 'onion' to refer to the four ESCP categories and how each was accompanied by its own set of criteria and contextualized examples to help both observer and observee in their (self) evaluation and reflective discussion:

If you think of those four elements, it's like an onion. You've got those four on the front [Engage, Support, Challenge and Progress], then some mixed sub-criteria under that and then under that layer you've got a kind of grid that shows what does effective practice in 'engaging' learners look like. So you could be having a discussion and I might say to you I think I am really good at 'engaging' students but I don't think I 'challenge' them all. So we'd then look at what comes under the onion of challenge and what does the classroom look like that's very effective and what does a less effective one look like and look at those descriptions etc. And often I think for me one of the most exciting bits of the process is you can start talking about where teachers felt they needed to develop before you observed them, rather than going through this whole process of going along and doing an observation with a one-size-fits-all set of criteria.

(O'Leary, 2013b: 85)

Penny's comments reinforced the importance of including a pre-observation meeting and how that could play a pro-active role in tutors' professional development. The final point she makes about how the ESCP model moves away from a restrictive 'one-size-fits-all set of criteria' and seeks to focus on the identified needs of individual practitioners is also highly significant as it highlights some of the flaws of such normalized models of observation previously discussed. In short, Rainbow College's ESCP model would appear to share many of the characteristics associated with expansive approaches to the use of observation and as such represent a powerful alternative to the hegemony of performative, graded observations.

Finally, when asked how staff at the college had received the ESCP model, Penny replied that, 'the feedback from staff has been overwhelmingly positive and a lot of people did genuinely experiment with something new'. However, she was keen to stress that its success was not purely as a result of changing the model of observation itself, but how that model was implemented and the way in which staff engaged with it:

It's not just about the model, it's about how a model is enacted and for me one of the things we still need to work on – and I think it is continuous – is developing the observers and their approach to the observations and the perception of some staff and working on the communication of it. So I think the model to me, if you had more time, is: spend a bit longer in your peer observation discussion – and I think that's a valuable element to keep, but it is time consuming, so it's how you make that most effective.

(O'Leary, 2013b: 85)

Penny's comment about needing to develop the 'perception' and 'approach' of observers and those observed to engaging with observation underlines how sustainable improvement is underpinned by an ongoing commitment to and investment in transforming the teaching and learning cultures of an institution and not just the introduction of a new model or initiative as a quick-fix solution.

## Concluding remarks

The challenge facing FE is how to move beyond the current hegemony that constrains the way in which many practitioners conceptualize and experience lesson observation. Performative observation has reached its threshold and now obstructs continued teacher learning and improvement. It is ironic that part of the original rationale for introducing graded observations was to weed out poor teachers, yet they have proven to be one of the least effective means of doing so. The level of inauthenticity inherent within observations has compromised the core validity and reliability of assessment, not to mention professional trust. If managers have to rely on episodic, summative observations of staff to be able to assess their professional capabilities, then clearly they are not managing their staff effectively in the first place. That can only be achieved through sustained relationships in which managers regularly observe and talk to their staff, and draw on a range of evidence when they appraise their professional performance and overall competence.

The test for managers such as Abdul, Cristina, Molly and Penny is therefore how to capture and demonstrate the tangible impact of these counter-hegemonic practices on improvements in teaching in a system that seems wedded to managerialist positivism. Efforts need to concentrate on unlocking the potential of observation to stimulate the sustained professional development of teachers. No longer should observation be seen as a predominantly summative assessment tool or disciplinary mechanism to be used episodically. It should be instead a method of inquiry that facilitates open, ongoing professional dialogue based on self-reflection, action research, feedback, peer coaching and experiential learning. Only then can the profession begin to reclaim observation as an empowering tool in the growth and professional development of teachers. However, this will only happen if teachers are encouraged to 'dance' freely in their classrooms, to experiment and to expose their practice to others in the common pursuit of furthering their understanding of the complex processes of teaching and learning, without the fear of punitive surveillance systems.

## References

Department for Education (2010) *The Importance of Teaching: The schools white paper*. London: DfE.

Foucault, M. (1977) *Discipline and Punish: The birth of the prison*. London: Allen Lane.

Gordon, C. (ed.) (1980) *Michel Foucault: Power/Knowledge–selected interviews and other writings 1972–1977*. Brighton: Harvester.

Gramsci, A. (1971) *Selections from the Prison Notebooks of Antonio Gramsci*. London: Lawrence and Wishart.

Institute for Learning (2012) *Leading Learning and Letting Go: Building expansive learning environments in FE*. London: IfL.

O'Leary, M. (2012) 'Exploring the role of lesson observation in the English education system: A review of methods, models and meanings'. *Professional Development in Education*, 38 (5), 791–810.

— (2013a) 'Expansive and restrictive approaches to professionalism in FE colleges: the observation of teaching and learning as a case in point'. *Research in Post-Compulsory Education*, 18 (4), 348–64.

— (2013b) *Developing a National Framework for the Effective Use of Lesson Observation in Further Education*. Project report for UCU. Online. www.ucu.org.uk/media/pdf/i/q/ucu_lessonobsproject_nov13.pdf (accessed 20 June 2014).

— (2014) *Classroom Observation: A guide to the effective observation of teaching and learning*. London: Routledge.

Smith, R., and O'Leary, M. (2013) 'New public management in an age of austerity: Knowledge and experience in Further Education'. *Journal of Educational Administration and History*, 45 (3), 244–66.

'FE gave me the chance to progress in a subject that I want to have as a career one day.'

Nathan Roberts

# Building Colleges for the Future: What the ugly sisters have to tell us about FE

*Rob Smith*

'Five-stepping with the other four hundred round and round Westminster Abbey, Lenina and Henry were yet dancing in another world – the warm, the richly coloured, the infinitely friendly world of soma-holiday. How kind, how good-looking, how delightfully amusing every one was!'

(Aldous Huxley)

Twenty years after the incorporation of FE colleges, to claim that marketization has brought with it an obsession with appearance seems like stating the obvious. We have the corporate logos, the production of annual glossy marketing materials and even a few attempts to introduce uniforms for staff (*Daily Mail*, 2009). But in addition to these examples, marketization has also had an impact on the places and the buildings where students learn and teachers work, and a government-backed scheme has made visible the architectural language of 'FE-incorporated'. What is striking in this is that despite the (market) freedom of college principals to plan and organize their employees and their educational provision as they see fit, many FE-incorporated new-builds look extremely similar from the outside.

This chapter draws on a range of data – including interviews with teachers and managers – to explore the impact of this new FE architecture on different stakeholders. The findings are that the glossy and glassy exteriors offered up to the public gaze are a triumph of form over function – they conceal the ugly truth of education reduced to a production-line accreditation system in which the self-interest of colleges-as-corporations comes first. Furthermore, the new architecture of FE-incorporated communicates the assimilation of students and teachers into a commodified fantasy in which educational relationships are pushed closer to those found in a shopping mall than in a classroom. As in the world of the fairy tale, status, prestige and power are signified by showiness in the market place and showiness in the Cinderella sector is a façade that conceals the threat commodification poses to the authentic personal and social relationships FE teachers strive to achieve.

## Context

Had it not been for the financial crisis of 2007–8, the FE estate in England would have been transformed over the last five years. The building that has gone ahead, a fraction of what might have taken place, provides insight into what we have (narrowly) escaped. If you were flying over different cities in England and trying to locate FE colleges from the air, they would be easy to pick out: huge glass-sided monoliths, probably nestled between landscaped plazas, their entrances leading to a cavernous atrium containing shops, a cafeteria and open learning spaces.

A typical exterior showing an extensive glazed façade. In this case, the atrium/entrance hall attracts the public gaze.

The glass-sided transparency of these buildings communicates their 'legibility' (Scott, 1998) to onlookers and these panopticon tendencies suggest an internal organization of lived-in space. The externalities of FE then, the foyer-ism and atria-addiction that have become such prevalent architectural features, supposedly fulfil the function of attracting custom to the colleges through ostentation. Behind this, however, they communicate something about how the relationship between institution and student is imagined.

This chapter explores how the architectural model of FE that has emerged over the 20 years since incorporation reflects key aspects of the marketization of the sector, in particular, the cultural representation of the college-as-corporation, the dominance of managerialist positivism

(Smith and O'Leary, 2013) in response to market accountability, and the objectification of FE students as funding fodder.

Since incorporation, successive governments have developed FE into something more than the handmaiden of British industry. Instead, FE has been used within a polity discourse that seeks to redefine the relationship between education and work, with a specific emphasis on young people. What I am suggesting is that FE has been cast in an ideological role that communicates a set of conservative and neoliberal views about education, specifically a commodified vision of education-for-the-purposes-of-employment. This ideological enterprise shapes identities to the extent that it appears to view students as figures in a commercial landscape in much the same way as Disney seeks to 'turn children into consumers and construct commodification as a defining principle of children's culture' (Giroux, 1994: 69). As the hard-driven servant of policy makers, FE has been subjected to a string of new strategies and curriculum initiatives. So if FE is a Cinderella sector, its duties are not established and routine, instead it has had to adapt to an ever-changing set of duties with the standard of its work continually scrutinized.

The buildings that FE students are educated in tell a connected story. The old FE building stock was a mixture of faded Victorian grandeur, post-war urban expansion with (often badly joined-up) piecemeal additions from the 1960s, 70s and 80s. Colleges opened annexes and outlets wherever there was a need, sometimes in repurposed community buildings. In the run-up to incorporation, there was a localism and a pragmatism in that the courses being delivered and the needs being met were perceived to be more important than a branded experience. But an increasing focus on FE as the vanguard sector in a competitive and marketized global skills race has meant a big change in the FE estate in the past five years.

In a publication entitled *World Class Buildings: Design Quality in Further Education,* the now defunct Learning and Skills Council (LSC) gave a hint of different ingredients in the architectural image envisioned for FE:

> With good design, the seminar and conference rooms, learning areas, staff accommodation, catering facilities and social areas in modern colleges could have the same effect as the design features that draw people into supermarkets, regional shopping centres and unique environments like the Eden project in Cornwall.
>
> (LSC, 2005: 6)

The sense the reader gets of the meaning of design in the passage above is of the college as something more akin to a convention centre than an educational institution. The rationale can be best described as theme-park logic: that grandeur, newness and glass are essential to attract footfall.

The current era of FE architecture began in 2007 when the LSC launched an investment programme that tied the development of the FE estate nationally to sustainability. The aim was 'to improve the quality of the FE estate, allowing colleges and sixth forms to better meet the needs of learners, employers and communities' (LSC, 2007a). But this focus on needs soon morphed into an initiative in which the old FE stock was replaced with new 'landmark' and 'flagship' buildings: structures of steel and glass, often featuring carefully designed social spaces. Furthermore, the initial emphasis on 'more sustainable' FE buildings developed a year later into an ambitious national programme where sustainability was a minor feature.

The LSC's 'Building Colleges for the Future' (BCF) programme (launched March 2008) was the FE version of a schools building programme – 'Building Schools for the Future' – that was introduced by New Labour in 2003. This was a scheme 'intended to point forwards to educational and social visions for the twenty-first century' (Mahony and Hextall, 2013: 866). The financial underpinnings of the project are eye-watering: in spring 2009, 75 colleges had projects with approval in principle and the total LSC grants these involved were £2.6 billion (AoC, n.d.). While little has been written about the FE scheme, according to Mahony *et al.* (2011: 346), 'From its inception, the BSF programme has been clearly located within an education policy context in which enhanced skills and knowledge are deemed to play a key role in the global dynamics of economic competition between states.'

Mahony *et al.* also cite the Department for Education and Skills as identifying a direct link between 'state-of-the-art' learning environments and the improvement of standards. 'Our research, and the increasing number of case studies that are becoming available, show a clear link between capital investment and improvements in school standards' (DfES, 2003: 4).

In a nutshell, the equation goes like this: new and 'better' buildings = better results = a more skilled workforce = a more competitive economy. Woolner *et al.* (2007) undertook a review of literature from the last 40 years and were unable to discern any link between these elements. Nonetheless, and whatever we may think about such a reductive and simplistic formula, this then was the ball for which 'FEnderella' was being groomed.

Unfortunately for colleges, the financial crisis of 2007–8 resulted in BCF being frozen in December 2008 after the money ran out. A few colleges with projects underway had to seek special dispensation to continue. But while BCF echoed BSF rhetoric about the impact of the physical environment on 'building participation rates, retention rates and attainment' (LSC, 2008: 2), it also had distinct differences. There was the skills agenda at its heart, focused on meeting the specialized demand of local industry and employers: 'To match the scale of the ambitions of Lord Leitch's report, it is essential that specialist FE facilities are cutting-edge and state-of-the-art, and that the FE estate is modernised accordingly' (ibid.: 21), in order to 'benefit generations of learners to come, meet the skills needs of employers and act as a catalyst for community regeneration' (ibid.: 1). Within the plans there is also an assumption about the reduction in size of the estate in response to a fall in projected student numbers and the development of 'more modern teaching and learning methods (such as information and learning technology (ILT)-led open learning)' (ibid.: 23). In these terms, the policy context for the current (much reduced) crop of newly built college campuses was set.

## Glass slippers or the ugly sisters?

From the outside, the new-build colleges are impressive. The exteriors of most of the new college buildings are dominated by glass. Glass walls symbolize, we might imagine, transparency, clear sightedness or perhaps the college as a hothouse of learning. Above all they 'showcase the College's … functions' (Broadway Malyan, n.d.) to the surrounding area. In psychoanalytic terms, glass symbolizes transformation (Singh, 2008: 11), which fits with a consumerist ethic that commodifies education as some kind of glossy and superficial identity-enhancing product. The opposite of the Masonic Lodge that seeks to maintain the secrecy of its membership with blanked out windows, these colleges' glass walls are an aspect of the buildings as physical display, as the colleges market themselves to their local communities. Within colleges (and other marketized public institutions) you sometimes hear talk of outward-facing documents – this is FE argot meaning documents that present a favourable image of the institution; the use of glass is an architectural expression of a college's outward-facing culture. Its glass frontage operates literally as 'a "window" for the college's professional academies' (Dyer, n.d.).

The 1990s saw the growth of 'foyerism' in colleges – the improvement of entrance areas to facilitate a greater emphasis on security and to provide an appropriate and branded outward-facing image to the public and other customers. The foyers of BCF buildings have, however, undergone steroidal development. The foyer has become an atrium often several storeys high and usually behind a glazed façade. More than an expanded foyer, they are reminiscent of a covered railway ticket hall or perhaps an airport terminal.

They are social spaces often overlooked by a cafeteria, a hair salon and a restaurant with staircases radiating outwards to the teaching areas. On a normal college day, they are filled with the kind of hustle and bustle you might find in any busy public, or commercial, space. Indeed, it's unsurprising that the architects for one of the colleges in the sample specialize in building shopping malls.

This flagship college building with its distinctive styling is situated alongside retail park development.

But how has BCF 'improved the quality of the FE estate … to better meet the needs of learners'? The next section draws on some data from research into the impact of new-build colleges on teaching and learning and on the social interactions between staff and between students. I gathered data on four different colleges in the West Midlands area (Southern College, Western College, Cherrytree College and Municipal College). All had had new-builds in the last three years. I used a 'live methods' (see Back and Puwar, 2013) approach that allowed me to draw data from multiple sources: interviews with an opportunistic sample of participants (more than 20 teachers, managers, student teachers), photographs, field observation, email exchanges, telephone conversations, and a videoed discussion. All of these are wrapped in an ethnographic envelope as I was drawing on relationships and my practice as a teacher educator in FE settings, established over a decade. To that extent, I consider myself an insider (Sikes and Potts, 2008) and an equal participant in the research process.

## Colleges for the Future: practitioners' views

The emphasis here is on empirical evidence. How have practitioners and students experienced these new-builds as places in which they teach and learn? From the outset, it is important to note that teachers and students of subjects which had bespoke accommodation provided (such as motor vehicle) regarded these new-builds in a positive light because in many cases their teaching accommodation replicated working environments. However, the majority of views from staff and students of classroom-based subjects expressed repeated concerns linked to the new buildings.

### *Atrium and market image*

Most participants regarded the atria positively. However, these atria had had negative impacts: they took up space that could have better been used for classrooms, and the noise levels within them could make teaching difficult in any adjoining classroom.

The first of these can be accounted for by the inflexibility of single-site new-builds, meaning that staff and students in two of the four newly built colleges experienced accommodation problems after the move to new premises (in one case leading to social spaces being used as classrooms). This might also be related to the increased focus on formulae that rigidly link floor space and student numbers (see LSC, 2007b). One rationale for the relocation of a multi-campus college to a single flagship building is that this enables the establishment of a branded identity. Unfortunately, this may also involve a reduction in teaching accommodation.

On the second point, the views of Kristos, a lecturer at Western College, provide a flavour:

> [Student services] organize steel bands and things like that. I like steel bands but when you're trying to teach in any of the classrooms that overlook the atrium, with a steel band going on in the background ... even with the windows and walls, the noise generated is just phenomenal.

The issue may be with soundproofing. However, the college in question had many classrooms with windows (which could not be opened, it has to be said) overlooking the atrium. In this case though, the social use of the atrium has taken on unintended significance – rather than simply providing a funnelling conduit into classrooms and learning spaces. It has taken on a life of its own, a student-centred life in which it has become a destination in its own right, not merely a corridor leading to more enclosed spaces.

Moreover, this new spatial identity abrades the teaching and learning functions of the college premises.

## Social learning spaces

The question of what is meant by learning spaces and the eliding of these with social spaces into the hybrid social learning spaces also requires commentary. The proliferation of these spaces in colleges – and they were a feature of each of the new-builds in this study – connects to an important policy current that sees education as being content-based and teaching as knowledge transmission. This view of education encourages a perception that providing students with internet access will automatically improve learning. These spaces can be seen as an extension of the shopping mall / atria and as such position students in particular ways. Social interaction between people in these spaces is factored in; sustained periods of concentration, focus and thinking are, however, unlikely to be achieved. The suggestion here is that learning has been equated with internet browsing and these areas provide an experience analogous to window-shopping. Another issue is that these spaces are vulnerable to encroachment when there are not enough classrooms.

Dhara at Southern College explains:

> One very large room in the [subject] area was a real problem and teachers did some team teaching and wore microphones to actually deliver the session. I never saw this but I believe it caused problems for other classes that were being taught. I did observe a session up there and it was like being in a busy railway station, even without the microphones!

The evocation of another kind of public space, this time a railway station, is instructive. Interestingly though, this time the multi-functionality of the space has led managers to utilize it for teaching and learning. In so doing they have re-conceptualized the classroom as a transport hub and shopping-mall hybrid, and teaching as a distorted tannoy announcement, with students reduced to baffled and discomfited commuters.

The hybridizing of social space and learning space: noise levels make
the use of such open areas for teaching problematic.

## Reduced resources for staff

In three of the four colleges researched, teachers reported that the move
to new premises also coincided with a reduction in amenities for staff. In
two colleges, while senior staff had designated car parking spaces, staff's
customary travel arrangements to work were also disrupted. Harpreet at
Cherrytree College commented:

> There's also no car parking for staff. They must pay and display
> across on the wasteland ... This has caused uproar with local

residents because staff park on the streets because they don't want to pay and display. People have got tickets because sometimes the machine doesn't work. So you can imagine the atmosphere in the morning…

This is where any analogy between new-build FE colleges and shopping malls breaks down, as the lack of parking impacts on staff and students alike. Travel to these colleges was necessary for staff and students, often from many miles across the region. While any institutional encouragement to use public transport might be laudable, this was not supported for staff by any institutionally organized travel packages. This suggests a failure to comprehend how these colleges connect effectively with their users and to city living more broadly. Bizarrely, it also harks back to a pre-incorporation period when colleges more usually catered for students from local communities in the immediate vicinity.

A reduction of office space caused another erosion of teachers' pre-existing conditions. Shared desks (so called hot-desks) were often standard and in some cases teachers also had to work around photocopiers or, despite the extensive use of glass in the design of the building, strangely found themselves in offices with no windows. Dhara at Southern College stated:

> A major issue for me and many of my colleagues is not having access to any quiet space. None at all. It was impossible to work sometimes and this has increased teachers' workload considerably – many of us have commented that we have more work to do at home.

The removal of quiet workspace for teachers resonates with the use of learning spaces for students. While it may be an exaggeration to describe the resulting space as hostile to quiet working practices, it does rather seem as though the design of these buildings assumes learning work is a busy, social activity – at any rate, we are a long way from the studies, cloisters and hush of more traditional educational spaces.

### Smart architecture / rooms not fit for teaching

All the participants noted that teaching was not in the minds of the designers of these buildings. The shortcomings of these so-called smart buildings ranged from swipe-card room access that continually broke down necessitating propping doors open with a chair; motion sensor lighting that disabled effective use of smart boards to watch videos; very poor acoustics in classrooms due to multiple reflective surfaces; poor ventilation again necessitating propping open doors; furniture screwed to concrete floors that prevented effective group work; rooms that were oddly shaped – either long and thin or narrowing at one end. Most of these complaints supported an overall view on the part of teaching staff and (some) managers that the buildings' exterior impression was prioritized over the educational functionality of the interior.

## Temperature

Finally, there is an obvious consequence from having extensive exterior walls that are glazed. Below are three voices from different colleges:

> The temperature varies drastically on the same floor. Our staffroom is boiling hot and some classes are freezing … More staff are taking sick leave … [It] has undoubtedly had an impact on teaching and learning.
>
> (Dhara, Southern College)

> One side of the building can be kept cool. The other can't. There are issues in certain classes, you can't keep them cool enough. In the summer they become sweltering hot. In my office there's no air con – on this whole side of the building. Form takes precedence over function.
>
> (Charlie, Municipal College)

> You can't open the windows in most of the rooms. You can for those that aren't facing out of the building. So you are relying on the air conditioning … There were huge problems with that. They couldn't get the temperature right as it was supposed to be environmentally friendly. So it was supposed to be circulating the natural air naturally. But it didn't work. So everyone had to have their coat on it because it was freezing or it was roasting – one student nearly passed out.
>
> (Harpreet, Cherrytree College)

These passages demonstrate that the most basic considerations for both teachers and students are breached by the ostentatious imagery inherent in these colleges' glass façades. What's interesting in these accounts is the extent to which the smart building and the rooms have taken on an identity that is both remote and inaccessible to the individual interventions of teaching staff. Ventilation and temperature are no longer about simply opening a window (they don't open) but instead involve engagement with an opaque and complex computerized system that may or may not know the teacher is there. These new buildings are significant additional factors that influence the activities of teaching and learning that constitute these teachers' work.

Where does this leave teaching and teachers? It changes nothing. The industrial revolution was born out of spillover between workshops; the original technical institutes had little more than tables and chairs. The policy fixation with appearance and performativity is, ultimately, an expression of the performative nature of the political world from which it issues. The socially embedded moral purpose at the heart of teaching enables it, however, to transcend mere estate. Teachers are able to teach and historically have taught in garages, workshops, kitchens, on pavements, under trees – to that extent the BCF initiative is an outward-facing environmental inconvenience: within it, FE teachers will continue to nurture educational relationships just as they always have.

Overall, the evidence is strong that the cost of showcasing, of transparency, of flagship buildings designed by shopping-mall architects, has, in many cases, been detrimental to the needs of teachers and students. While the glass slipper looks spectacular, it doesn't actually fit Cinderella – it's also freezing cold on some days and swelteringly hot on others. If you get into it, using your swipe card, you may not be able to get back out.

## Conclusions

Finally, there is another and more significant problem with building FE colleges that resemble shopping malls. That is the emerging trend of the extinction of shopping malls in the US – a trend that has every chance of spreading to the UK. Malls are associated with an older generation of shoppers and some are closing because of catastrophic decline in footfall (Howe, 2013). This is due to the different buying habits of the Gen Xers – young people who have grown up as consumers who make purchases via the internet. The predictions are that this change in buying habits is going to influence the human geography and architecture of our cities over the next ten years. City centres will have to develop beyond their orientation around retail and rediscover their purpose as environments that engender social cohesion (a function long recognized as an important aspect of pre-marketized FE). While the Building Colleges of the Future programme has produced mall-like buildings with a 60-year life span, colleges will have to reimagine how their buildings are used if they are not to be the victims of their sell-by date.

Here is a final thought about the kind of social cohesion these atria are engendering. Many participants spoke about the use and function of the atria and how they encouraged young people to gather. Kristos stated:

The biggest problem with the atrium is the volume of students that are down there from 8.30 in the morning through to the evening. It's used as a social area . When they first come into the college, people find it intimidating ... It looks unprofessional.

Another participant observed:

We herd the students and control their behaviour through a heavy security presence ... I have a thing about social-learning spaces. If you make these spaces where [students] are not bored and are actively engaged you won't need such a security presence. If you can, give them some interesting things to do in the social spaces. You can give them something with some educational value. So they can learn and be social as opposed to just giving them some chairs and tables.

Both participants are suggesting that college students are being encouraged to congregate, and the colleges find these architecturally integrated social spaces resistant to the FE-incorporated brand and undermining of the cultures of compliance staff are forced to endure. This suggests that the relationship between educational space and student is less deterministic than co-constitutive. FE students and teachers are as able to produce their own meanings within these new-builds as they are to have meanings imposed on them. When student awareness of the costs of the current hegemony around the commodification of education becomes more focused, it may be that these hybrid 'social and learning' spaces become the crucibles in which new collective and resistant student identities are forged.

# References
AoC (n.d.) *Capital Projects*. Online. http://tinyurl.com/l2mjbde (accessed 14 January 2015).

Back, L., and Puwar, N. (eds) (2013) *Live Methods*. London: Wiley-Blackwell.

Broadway Malyan (n.d.) *Bournville College*. Online. www.broadwaymalyan.com/projects/regions/uk/bournville-college (accessed 13 July 2013).

*Daily Mail* (2009) 'Now TEACHERS told to wear clothes that co-ordinate in new uniform crackdown.' Online. http://tinyurl.com/l7ea5rz (accessed 28 April 2014).

DfES (2003) *Building Schools for the Future: Consultation on a new approach to capital investment*. London: DfES.

Dyer (n.d.) *Walsall Business and Learning Campus*. Online. www.groupdyer.co.uk/project/1984/ (accessed 13 July 2013).

Giroux, H.A. (1994) 'Animating youth: The Disneyfication of children's culture'. *Socialist Review*, 94 (3), 23–55. Online. www.lafayetteschools.org/tfiles/folder1077/Giroux.pdf (accessed 30 April 2014).

Howe, N. (2013) 'Are malls becoming extinct?' *USA Today* (18 December).

LSC (2005) *World Class Buildings: Design quality in Further Education.* Online. http://readingroom.lsc.gov.uk/lsc/2005/research/commissioned/world-class-buildings.pdf (requires subscription) (accessed 29 April 2014).

LSC (2007a) *LSC launch strategy for building greener colleges of the future.* Online. http://tinyurl.com/mjph3rl (accessed 17 July 2013).

LSC (2007b) *Guidance for Further Education Colleges on the Management of Floor Space.* Online. http://readingroom.lsc.gov.uk/lsc/national/Floorspace_Guidance_-_02_05_07_doc_v2__2_.pdf (requires subscription) (accessed 1 May 2014).

LSC (2008) *Building Colleges for the Future.* Online. http://www.eauc.org.uk/sorted/building_colleges_for_the_future (accessed 14 January 2015).

Mahony, P., Hextall, I., and Richardson, M. (2011) 'Building schools for the future: Reflections on a new social architecture'. *Journal of Education Policy*, 26 (3), 341–60.

Mahony, P., and Hextall, I. (2013) 'Building schools for the future: Transformation for social justice or expensive blunder?' *British Educational Research Journal* 39 (5), 853–71.

Scott, J.C. (1998) *Seeing Like a State: How certain schemes to improve the human condition have failed.* New Haven: Yale University Press.

Sikes, P., and Potts, A. (eds) (2008) *Researching Education from the Inside: Investigations from within.* London: Routledge.

Singh, V. (2008) 'Cinderella's Slippers: The dichotomy of fur and glass'. MA essay, Simon Fraser University.

Smith, R., and O'Leary, M. (2013) 'New public management in an age of austerity: Knowledge and experience in Further Education'. *Journal of Educational Administration and History*, 45 (3), 244–66.

Woolner, P., Hall, E., Higgins, S., McCaughey, C., and Wall, K. (2007) 'A sound foundation? What we know about the impact of environments on learning and the implications for Building Schools for the Future'. *Oxford Review of Education,* 33 (1), 47–70.

'FE gave me a second chance to study something I love at a higher level, gaining knowledge and experiences that I will carry into my future career.'

Heidi Billingsley

# Chapter 8

# Reframing professionalism and reclaiming the dance
## Dan Taubman

> *'And those who were seen dancing were thought to be insane by those who could not hear the music.'*

(Friedrich Nietzsche)

This chapter arose out of work undertaken as the Senior Education Official (Further Education) at the University and College Union (UCU). It followed a dispute with the Institute for Learning (IfL), the then professional body for teaching and training staff in the FE and skills sector. This dispute took place in 2011 following the announcement that IfL members would have to pay the IfL membership fee themselves. From the point in 2007 when IfL membership became mandatory, the fee had been paid by the Department of Business, Innovation and Skills (BIS). UCU members and others, while initially welcoming the creation of IfL, felt that it had no added value for them and that it was just another piece of unnecessary bureaucracy. UCU held a ballot on refusing to pay the fee, which was supported, and eventually around 120,000 of IfL's 200,000 members refused to pay the membership fee. The subsequent Lingfield review of professionalism (Lingfield, 2012) recommended that IfL membership no longer be mandatory. As the UCU official who had been the link to IfL and had sat on the IfL Board since its inception, I began to ponder: if UCU members rejected the IfL and its concept of professionalism, this did not mean they were not professionals. So what kind of professionalism would they accept?

The central argument of this chapter is that the professionalism of all education workers has to be reclaimed from the current neoliberal grip exerted on all aspects of education. Traditional definitions of professionalism identify a specific group of workers with a defined body of knowledge and expertise and a set of values and ethics that underpin the delivery of certain services. It was through the exercise of these services, within an ethical framework, that professions and professionals were allowed to act autonomously and exercise their judgement. In traditional professions the state refrained from overt supervision and control, which became known as the professional mandate or bargain. A reclaimed and reframed professionalism will create a new professional bargain not only with the state, but also with students. This new professionalism rests on a set of values including equality, social justice, democracy, sustainability, well-being and creativity. These are grounded within a belief in people's ability to transform themselves and to transcend their situations and the society in which they live.

Professionalism in education is under serious attack from a culture of managerialism. There is a lack of respect for the expertise, views and commitment of professional staff and the imposition of ever-increasing workloads. Education and learning have been commodified: they are being bought and sold. Market forces and competition drive the current education system, backed up by powerful state tools such as inspection and funding. Models of professionalism associated with this impoverished version of education emphasize compliance and regulation. By contrast, the concept of professionalism set out here is an attempt to get the balance right, between giving a central role to the voice of education workers, while recognizing wider society's legitimate interest in standards and accountability.

## Definitions of professionalism

There are many different typologies of professionalism, the main three being traditional, managerialist and democratic. Traditional professionalism has a distinct body of knowledge, skills, attributes and expertise, acquired through an extended and systematic preparation, usually in an institutional setting, and enhanced through continuous professional development (CPD). Underpinning values and ethics may be set out in a code of professional behaviour. This has meant that traditional professions such as medicine and the law were accorded a degree of autonomy and freedom from external scrutiny by the state. This created a framework of accountability to the state and to the client – in the case of education, the student – and known as the professional mandate or bargain. In reclaiming and reframing professionalism, this mandate has to be formulated anew, because this traditional professionalism does not take account of the current social and political contexts of marketization and privatization of public services.

Two competing discourses remain, shaping the professionalism and professional identity of education workers: managerialist and democratic professionalism. The current predominant paradigm in education is of neoliberal managerialism. Managerialism rests on two distinct claims: that efficient management can solve any problem and that the practices that are appropriate for the conduct of private-sector enterprises can also be applied to the public sector. Under this approach professionalism becomes divorced from the social and political context in which it is practised. Rather than evolving from the lived experience and knowledge of the participants, professionalism is defined by top-down regulation and compliance. The status and power of professionals becomes increasingly dependent on their ability to cast goals and objectives in appropriate terms.

Managerialist professionalism is about control by managers. It is a rational-legal form of authority with bureaucratic, hierarchical structures of decision making and standardization of work procedures and practices. The relationship between employer and professional shifts from one based on trust to one based on supervision, assessment and audit. This also affects relations between practitioners and students, with the student becoming a customer; organizational forms of regulation replace trust relationships between practitioner and student. In these circumstances professional cohesion and mutual cooperation are undermined and competition threatens team working and collegial support.

Against this, Sachs (1999), Whitty (in Cunningham, 2008: 44) and others such as the RSA have put forward the concept of a democratic or activist professionalism and identity. Democratic professionalism reconceptualizes professionalism in the light of developments in education, and especially in teaching and learning, and takes account of the social and political context that education professionals are now facing. Democratic professionalism seeks to demystify professional work and build alliances between educational professionals and other members of the institution's workforce and external stakeholders, including students, parents and members of the wider community. A democratic professionalism encourages the development of collaborative cultures in the broadest sense. It argues that the education professional has a responsibility that extends beyond the single classroom, including contributing to the institution, learners and to the wider educational system, as well as to the collective responsibilities of the professionals to a broader social agenda. Indeed, under democratic professionalism, this broader agenda becomes part of the professional agenda.

## Education and professionalism now

Since the mid-1970s, however, there have been dramatic changes in education policy and, linked to these, the nature of educational professionalism has begun to change. There have been sustained attacks on the public sector. These attacks have taken the form of funding cuts and accusations that public-sector professionals were abusing their professional autonomy and trust for narrow sectoral interests. These attacks also contained a critique of public-sector management. The answer of governments since the 1980s has been to subject the public sector, including education, to market forces and competition, coupled with increasing amounts of state regulation and surveillance through quality-assurance schemes and inspection. The public sector and education have increasingly aped the forms and practices of business; meeting targets, student throughput and income generation take precedence. Teaching became individualistic and competitive, controlled and regulated through externally defined standards and targets.

Since the Education Reform Act (1988) there has been a steady and sustained shift away from reliance on professional judgements as the basis of accountability, to accountability through external agencies and measures. Policy and decision making have been centralized while local government's role in education has almost vanished. Central government sets the curriculum and the examination, assessment and qualifications regimes. There are increasing numbers of autonomous education institutions funded centrally. It defines quality and quality performance for both institutions and individuals, and publicizes the former through performance tables, which rank institutions. The Conservative-Liberal Democrat Coalition Government has achieved a further and deeper level of marketization and privatization by opening up public education services and institutions to the private sector. The government has intensified its drive to make every school an autonomous institution, freed from democratic control and accountability to the local authority, as it tries to create a kind of fantasy version of education in the 1950s, which is fragmented, elitist and hierarchical.

The growth of market forces and the accompanying spread of managerialism in education have profound implications for education and education professionalism. Standardized criteria now feed into the framework of targets and indicators that schools, colleges and individual teachers must work to, and the new assessment regimes provide a wealth of performance data for managers at all levels of the system.

The consequences of the development of managerialism in education are limits to professional agency. It encourages uncritical compliance and challenges professional identity. It reduces the time teachers have to connect with, care for and attend to the needs of individual learners. This diminishes teachers' sense of motivation. Assessment becomes the formal auditing of pupils' learning with learner outcomes set and monitored rigorously by senior management. Performance-related pay links career progression to learner outcomes. Audit-based external accountability constrains teacher autonomy, replacing it with a contrived collegiality and surveillance. It must also be noted that the Coalition Government has undertaken a massive programme of deregulation. Teacher professionalism itself is progressively and deliberately being subverted, with the English professional body for school teachers being abolished and that for FE lecturers being made non-mandatory, and subsequently dissolving itself. Qualifications in teaching are no longer required to work in FE and in an increasing number of schools.

The drive for managerialism in education also produces a deeper and more insidious malaise: what Ball calls performativity. This describes the way that managerialism and performance-management systems work on individuals by convincing them to be more effective, to work on themselves to improve or else to feel guilty or inadequate. Performativity works most powerfully when it is inside our heads and our souls. This leads to a general sense of personal insecurity and a loss of meaning, in what individuals do and what is important. The impact of the internalization of managerialist values is to re-orient pedagogical, scholarly and professional activities to performance outputs that can be measured. There is a deflection of attention away from aspects of social, educational, emotional and moral development that are not immediately measurable. Professionals' perceptions and experience of their work change, as does their satisfaction that derives from the deployment of their professional expertise and skills. Their sense of moral purpose and feeling of responsibility for their pupils and students becomes distorted. As Ball puts it, 'commitments are sacrificed for impression' (Ball, 2008: 54). Professionals become reinvented as units whose performance and productivity are constantly measured and audited. Accountability becomes yet another weapon to bind the professional more tightly to a set of values, about which they may feel profoundly uneasy. Ball states it thus:

> We make ourselves calculable rather than memorable. Experience ends up counting for nothing and productivity everything. The professional has to keep up, meet newer and ever more diverse targets in which they collude in setting. Appraisal can become a form of confession where the professional is encouraged to confront her/his supposed weaknesses and receive absolution through professional development, in order to become more productive.
>
> (Ball, 2008: 52)

He concludes that:

> All of this takes its toll; performativity comes to be inscribed in our bodies as well as our minds making us anxious, tired and stressed. It individualizes and fragments the issues around

> professionalism and leaves us to struggle along with our doubts and fears. The result of this is to break down our defences against marketisation and managerialism. That's its intent.
>
> (Ball, 2008: 56)

Marketization and privatization change what is important, valuable and necessary in education. The market sets the moral and ethical cultures for producers and consumers, rather than educational professionals and their learners. Both the educational institution and its staff have to adjust to a culture in which self-interest predominates. 'The private sector is now embedded into the heart and sinews of the state education services at all levels, intertwined into the day-to-day business of decision making, infrastructural development, capacity building and service delivery' (Ball, 2008: 63). Managerialism means that judgements about education are almost entirely made through quantifiable measures such as money spent, exams achieved and lessons rated as good. The consequence of this will be damaged and stunted lives, thwarted aspirations, a waste of talents and static social mobility. A reframed and reconfigured concept of professionalism aims to reassert a set of values that educational professionals can subscribe to and use in their work.

## Issues in professionalism

A new professionalism will not be unproblematic. It will have to define itself, state its position and resolve some key issues, specifically around professional values, the reclamation of autonomy and the fostering of specialist knowledge and expertise.

### 1. Values

Managerialism has inserted a set of values to sustain it, which are based on market forces. These are not educational values. Conflicts and tensions between these managerial values and the education values that professionals hold are destructive at both a systems and individual level. Ball (2008) talks about it eating into the soul of the professional. New professional values will need to be built from the longstanding educational values of empowerment, equality of opportunity, inclusiveness and sustainability, as well as the liberation that the creation, dissemination and utilization of knowledge and learning bring to society and individuals.

The central features of ethical conduct, integrity and moral probity will remain part of a new professionalism. But the major changes in society mean growing complexity, uncertainty and unpredictability in the ways in which these attributes are deployed, which may undermine previous certainties in relation to professional practice. A new professionalism has to reinterpret these central features. It has to move away from the characteristics that accompanied traditional professionalism, which were often class based, privileged and patriarchal. It must also consciously seek to demystify professionalism and its activities. The educational values of this new professionalism comprehend that knowledge is not fixed, and allow the existence and validity of different views and beliefs. This makes for greater negotiation and acknowledgement of mutual experience by the professional, rather than reliance on a hierarchical model of expertise and authority which often rests on paternalistic assumptions of professional infallibility (Cunningham, 2008: 88). The new professional is prepared to struggle to understand complexity, and if necessary to tolerate ambivalence and discomfort.

Lunt (in Cunningham, 2008: 90–3) also suggests a number of underpinning and reframed principles and values that can inform this new professionalism. Thus competence and satisfactory performance become more provisional and accepted as things that are rarely static and unchanging. Traditional notions of professional competence carrying with them a lifelong licence to practise are no longer adequate or acceptable in a fast-changing world. Professionals need to learn from experience and ensure that their knowledge, skills and understanding are current.

Similarly the value of respect includes an ability to listen and an attempt to achieve greater equality and mutual understanding by endorsing the validity of students' views through a partnership approach. The new professionalism also means collaboration and teamwork with a different mode of relating to other professionals. It means respecting the inherent dignity of all, regardless of gender, culture, social class, ethnicity, nationality, religion, age, sexuality or perceived ability. Professionalism is then based on empathy, care and compassion.

Integrity is reframed to take in a realization of one's own values, prejudices, beliefs, limitations and fallibility. It means an ability and willingness to reflect on and use previous practice and the ability to reflect on professional relationships. Humility as a value accepts personal fallibility as part of the human condition. It is then possible for professionals to make mistakes, but learn from them. Finally, responsibility involves an acceptance of dilemmas inherent in professional work and the increased complexity of the current and future professional pupil–student relationships. Such values undermine traditional notions of expertise and the power relations behind this. This democratic professionalism will take these new progressive values and use them as a powerful defence against the encroachments of managerialism, marketization and privatization.

## 2. Autonomy

The autonomy of the professional, to be trusted to use their expertise and make judgements, especially in new situations, is one of the core elements of professionalism. In all aspects of current education, professional autonomy has been eroded to almost nothing. Increased surveillance of both institutions and individuals, combined with rigorous target setting, are producing mechanistic teaching and learning where the scope for professional activity and judgements is drastically reduced. This is reinforced by funding, quality assurance and inspection systems. Managerialism attempts to control, constrain and diminish forms of professional autonomy and sites of resistance. Government and its agencies, not practitioners, now create standards, which they view as unambiguous criteria for outcomes that can be translated into practice. Through specification of detail, performance criteria and outcomes, standards become tools in the reduction of professional autonomy. Education professionals have to reclaim their autonomy as part of a renegotiated professional bargain between professionals, the state, society and students. Such professional autonomy becomes an active concept that does not claim to be value and context free. It puts the political and social realities back into the discourse. The central tenet of this new education professionalism is that it is based in the lived experiences of education workers but its building blocks include communities of practice that bring together education professionals and other stakeholders within a set of jointly owned values.

## 3. Specialist knowledge and expertise

One of the underpinning elements of professionalism is the specialist knowledge, skills and understanding that professionals possess. This is what, in part, the professional bargain rests upon. This body of underpinning knowledge and expertise is, however, increasingly being challenged by what can be termed 'the information age' with its increasing access to electronic and digital sources of information. Access to what previously had been unchallenged knowledge and expertise can alter the relationships between the individual professional and the student, which may threaten longstanding notions of professional expertise and authority. With marketization and privatization there has been an accompanying growth in 'consumer' power which, it is said, will lead to a less deferential and better informed public. In a marketized age there is the ability for the parent or student to shop around. People no longer believe or are prepared to behave as though the professional knows best. In this globalized world in the age of information, knowledge and trust can be relative. In the 'knowledge society' everyone can be knowledgeable or at least informed to a certain extent. In this environment, claims for professional knowledge can be seen as self-interest, so the position of professionals as unassailable has become more fragile. Knowledge and expertise for this new professionalism will need to be open to challenge and will need to meet developments within the relevant field and within society. Specialist knowledge and expertise should derive from multiple elements of professionalism: that is, from knowledge of subject, discipline, and pedagogy, as well as knowledge of political, social and economic realities. This knowledge and expertise will have been acquired through both study and experience. Professionals' specialized knowledge and expertise will need to be open and shared for the common good. It must not become yet another commodity in the education and data marketplace. It will need to be developed democratically as part of a data and knowledge commonwealth. There will need to be networks of professionals whose expertise will be in the creation and interpretation of data, which will no longer be a secret garden, but be turned into really useful knowledge, used to influence and develop curricula and learning.

Alongside specialist knowledge a set of skills will be needed by the education professional that are essential for successful teaching and learning, such as the communication of ideas through presentation, promotion of interaction and discussion and giving feedback. These skills involve interpersonal and intrapersonal abilities. Specialist knowledge can be relative and provisional because it is dynamic and is continually growing. Knowledge and skills will also arise from practitioner networks and communities of practice, which will need to be nurtured. These will allow for the lateral exchange of ideas, views and experiences between professionals within a subject or discipline.

Education professionals within every education phase will need the freedom, within the law, to hold and express opinions, question and test established ideas and received wisdom, and present controversial or unpopular points of view. Educational professionals must be free to explore all appropriate knowledge and be free of undue and unnecessary external control. The underpinning ethics and values that education professionals hold is the bulwark against abuse, by the state, society and their students.

## A new professionalism

This new professionalism will be democratic. It will be built from collaborative, cooperative action between education professionals and other education stakeholders. This will encompass strategies for education development, skill development and work organization. The professional's responsibility will reach beyond the single site for learning, be it the classroom, lecture hall, laboratory or workshop. Democratic professionalism involves being sensitive to a range of stakeholders, some of whose voices have been silenced in traditional professionalism. It will include contributing to the institution, the wider education system and the wider community. It will embrace collective responsibilities, both to fellow professionals and students, and to other professions. It allows different viewpoints to build a more democratic education system and ultimately a more open, more democratic society.

This new professionalism will value individual and collective professional effort, and proactive engagement in challenging inequality and injustice. It will recognize threats to education in the changing political environment. It will include a responsibility to expand equalities of opportunities for all students so there are no barriers to everyone realizing their aspirations and extending their talents. This is not a neutral professionalism that seeks to defend narrow, sectarian, vested interests. It is active and dynamic and seeks to build a better and more humane society.

The new professionalism will need to rebuild trust among students, colleagues and the general public, so that the ability of professionals to make judgements about their own work is restored. The professional bargain will be reconfigured to allow the exercise of professionals' knowledge and skills according to an openly articulated set of values and ethics. In return, the public and the state can trust the profession. This is expressed in terms of autonomy for the professional, in her or his work, and a limit to the interference and micro-management by the state. It is through this bargain, where competence and integrity are exchanged for trust, that professional freedom will be free from unwarranted and unnecessary supervision and interference.

Professionals have to experiment with new approaches and techniques, to be critical about their own performance in relation to their objectives and those of their students. Professional formation and development are not clean linear movements. They can be jerky and untidy. To develop as an education professional requires a belief that improvements can be made. It also requires an open and inquiring mind – one that is interested in learning and in how to enable learning to occur. All of this requires time for reflection, updating and continuous development, both in subject knowledge and as teachers and educators.

## A new professional identity

The reclaimed and reframed democratic professionalism set out above will need new professional identities in the education workforce. One of the originators of the concept of democratic professionalism, Judyth Sachs, sets out an activist professional identity. Sachs characterizes this as arising from:

> The open flow of ideas, regardless of their popularity, which enable people to be as fully informed as possible. It is focused around faith in the individual and collective capacity of people to create possibilities for resolving problems. It uses critical reflection and analysis to evaluate ideas, problems and policies. It is concerned for the welfare of others and the common good ... It recognises the dignity and rights of individuals and minorities. This new democratic or activist professional identity understands that democracy is not so much an ideal to be pursued as an idealised set of values that must be lived and that must guide professional life.
>
> (Sachs, 1999: 149–61)

Activist professionals are concerned to reduce or eliminate exploitation, inequality and oppression. Accordingly the development of this identity is deeply rooted in principles of equity and social justice. Discussions around this concept of an activist professional identity involve the nurturing of communities of practice. These develop in larger contexts – historical, social, cultural, and institutional and with specific reference to resources and constraints. Within these communities there are various levels of expertise that should be seen as a shared set of professional resources. Communities of practice require sustained engagement, and at the same time demand discussion and debate to share meanings about both the subject and practice of education. These communities can involve both the engagement and stimulation of the imagination of professionals. This is fundamental to the development of an activist professional identity. This provides the conditions and the opportunities for the role of the activist professional to be legitimated, recognized and practised. Democratic professional identity provides the conditions for the development of communities of practices that are collegial, and negotiated. Communities of practice are primarily concerned with engaging with some activity, but also in figuring out how this fits into the broader scheme of things (Wenger, 1998). Communities of practice and an activist identity will exist alongside one another. They will reinforce and support each other. They can form and reform around specific issues or around other perhaps longer-standing issues within the subject. These communities need academic freedom to flourish, because this allows free debate and discussion.

From communities of practice within an education system that emancipates rather than constricts teachers and students there will be alliances between professionals and the wider communities that they seek to serve. The education professionals reconceive themselves as agents of change rather than victims of change. But it is not an easy path as the government's continuing neoliberal policies constantly threaten to undermine the professional's morale and the public's trust. The activist professional has to be aware of the changes and developments in education and learning. Many of these developments may be seen as a possible dilution of professionalism and practices. Others can, if engaged with and approached positively through the analysis that comes from democratic professionalism, be used for the immense benefit of students as well as education professionals.

## Conclusions

This chapter sets out a concept of professionalism for education workers that stems explicitly from their experiences, knowledge and needs: it is a radically different form of professionalism from the one that is dominant in these times of managerialism, marketization and privatization. It is concerned with education and learning as social and public goods, not items to be bought, sold and consumed. However, education professionals cannot achieve this on their own. Like the twelve dancing princesses they are not autonomous: they always have to operate both within and without the education state, and to dance at times subject to the jurisdiction of the king. Education professionals will need to use this new professionalism to explore new and different freedoms to the ones extolled by the government. They will be conceived as much more active, rather than being essentially passive and receptive. The new professionalism will be focused on freedoms for teachers to use their judgements, to experiment, to innovate and to dance in a way that enhances their students' lives and their wider communities.

## References

Ball, S. (2008) 'Performativity, privatisation, professionals and the state'. In Cunningham, B. (ed.) *Exploring Professionalism*. London: Institute of Education.

Cunningham, B. (ed.) (2008) *Exploring Professionalism*. London: Institute of Education.

Lingfield, R. (2012) *Professionalism in Further Education: Final report of the Independent Review Panel* (the Lingfield review). London: BIS.

Lunt, I. (2008) 'Ethical issues in professional life'. In Cunningham, B. (ed.) *Exploring Professionalism*. London: Institute of Education.

Sachs, J. (1999) 'Teacher professional identity: Competing discourses, competing outcomes'. *Journal of Education Policy*, 16 (2), 149–61.

Wenger, E. (1998) *Communities of Practice: Learning, meaning and identity*. Cambridge: Cambridge University Press.

Whitty, G. (2008) 'Changing modes of teacher professionalism: Traditional, managerial, collaborative and democratic'. In Cunningham, B. (ed.) *Exploring Professionalism*. London: Institute of Education.

'FE has changed my life. It enabled me to take steps towards achieving a dream I had never believed was attainable. It gave me the opportunity for self-belief and inspiration, with support and encouragement. FE made me believe in myself as someone of value. I am so happy and my quality of life is so much better for me and my children.'

Stephenie Wiggins

# 'The soldier danced with them unseen': Managerial resistance and collusion in FE
## Damien Page

> 'All the ills of mankind, all the tragic misfortunes that fill the history books, all the political blunders, all the failures of the great leaders have arisen merely from a lack of skill at dancing.'

(Molière)

## Introduction

At the heart of 'The Twelve Dancing Princesses' is a binary opposition, an opposition that has been well rehearsed within the academic literature. On the one hand, there is the power of the king, his regal mechanisms of control stretching to curtail the actions of his daughters and executing any who let him down. On the other hand, there are the princesses, resisting the imposition of royal identity and behaviours, sabotaging the king's strategies of surveillance by drugging his spies and escaping the confines of the castle and their imposed identities to participate in frivolity and merriment. From a labour process theory perspective, the king can be seen to appropriate the freedom of his daughters, attempting a colonization of their identity to produce royal clones in his own image. The princesses then retaliate, re-appropriating their freedom via clandestine acts of resistance to take back their autonomy and their identity. So far so straightforward, a tale of power and resistance.

Yet the presence of the soldier complicates matters. On one level, his role is unremarkable – he is hired to investigate the mystery of the princesses' worn-out shoes by spying on them. As such, he is an agent of the king, a tool in the subordination of the princesses and in this he proves to be a wily and skilled agent. However, while the king's instructions are clear, the soldier does not limit himself to the act of pursuit and surveillance: we are told he danced with the princesses while invisible and even drank their wine before they had a chance to quench their thirst. Not only did he participate in secret on the first night, he followed them for a further two nights, perhaps to confirm his findings but perhaps to 'watch the wonderful goings on' and prolong his peripheral engagement in the merriment. Each time he enacted a performance to facilitate his task: he pretended to drink the drugged wine and he pretended to be asleep, astute acts of impression management. At the end of each night's invisible participation, he returned to pretence so as not to be found out. The status of the soldier is therefore not straightforward. On the one hand, he is an agent of the king, a surveiller for the royal family and a collector of tokens of their guilt. On the other hand, he acts outside of his official role by covert participation in the resistance, dancing unseen by either the princesses or the king. Furthermore, by not reporting the dance after the first night, the soldier has a third role as colluder with the princesses, facilitating their dance for his own ends. From this perspective, as agent and resister, performer and colluder, the soldier is the perfect metaphor for the contemporary first and middle-tier manager in FE.

Much of the literature that focuses on FE retains the dichotomous model of power and resistance with autocratic senior leaders pursuing the financial imperative, appropriating time, labour and professional identity from the teaching workforce who, in turn, resist their subjugation via a range of strategies. There are the overt forms of resistance such as strike action, but also the more routine forms of resistance, the subtle subversions, disengagements and ambiguous accommodations (Prasad and Prasad, 1998), 'making out', in Burawoy's (1979) terms, as lecturers exploit the loopholes and work their way around the system. Yet this dichotomous approach to power and resistance often leads to the reification of one over the other, with one often becoming privileged in academic studies. Furthermore, this dichotomous approach frames every employee as either a manager or managed, as either one engaged in subjugation or one who is being subjugated. As such, managers are conceptually excluded from resistance – they can't simultaneously subjugate and resist subjugation. The reality, of course, is that management is not a homogeneous group and no more likely to acquiesce to corporate cloning than any other worker. Managers are just as likely to share in the subjugation of chalk-face workers, especially managers at the first and middle tiers who are the implementers rather than the architects of strategy. What is needed then is a dialectical approach to the consideration of power and resistance, an approach that moves away from the twentieth century's preoccupation with management as a science and focuses instead on the 'dilemmas, ambiguities, paradoxes, tensions and contradictions' (Collinson, 2014: 41) that exist within organizations. A dialectical approach – 'the dynamic interplay and articulation together of opposites' (Mumby, 2005: 23) – allows us to understand first and middle-tier managers as liminal, not just 'buffers' between two competing forces, but agentively moving between the enaction of power and the enaction of resistance, participating in and eschewing both in response to each particular situation they are faced with, simultaneously situational managers and situational resisters.

Yet the argument so far has been metaphorical and conceptual; what is needed is an examination of the realities of managerial resistance. As such, this chapter draws upon findings from a study of 27 first and middle-tier managers from four large general FE colleges. Reflecting a broad spectrum of subject areas, from carpentry to A levels, the participants were interviewed three times over the course of a year and were observed in team meetings. The research began by focusing on the role of first-tier manager, a role largely neglected in the academic literature. What became apparent very quickly was that this role was extremely varied, moving from a teacher-as-coordinator position in some colleges, to middle management with first-tier management responsibilities in others. What also became apparent was that the title of management did not mean identification with management and that resistance was an essential part of their work and organizational life, not only to counter subjugation but also as a means of getting the job done and clawing back their professional autonomy.

## Managerial resistance and collusion

One of the most onerous tasks experienced by non-senior managers was the endless reporting and data collection required by senior managers and there were a range of resistant responses. One of the most common was to not respond, to merely ignore the requests. John was Curriculum Manager for Painting and Decorating and received an instruction from his college's human resources department to conduct a return-to-work interview with a member of his team who had had flu. For John, this was not part of his role, regardless of what his job description said and he was concerned that such a task may damage his relationship with his team-member:

> I've now got to interview him about [his illness] but I just don't really think that's my job, it's either personnel or the [middle] manager's job, you know. It's still sitting on my desk at the moment … so I might just ignore it and it probably will go away.

Yet instructions were also frequently ignored when they challenged the professional values of managers and teachers, especially those that increased surveillance. In Abbie's college, first-tier managers were required to distribute new student voice questionnaires that asked students to grade their teachers from unsatisfactory to outstanding. Appalled at the attempt to involve students in the surveillance of teachers and worried about the reaction of her team, Abbie ignored the instruction and threw them away:

> We just put it very quietly into the bin, just didn't do it. We didn't ever say 'we're not going to do this', we just didn't do it.

In most managerial contexts, ignoring requests from senior managers usually risks disciplinary action; first-tier and middle managers in FE, however, relied on their detailed understanding of the culture and systems of their organizations – FE colleges, they understood, were forgetful organizations. Not in the sense of failing to retain knowledge that is usually described as organizational amnesia but in the very literal sense that senior managers made so many repetitive requests for information, they simply forgot what they had asked of whom. Non-senior managers, wily and agentive, merely exploited this forgetfulness and even tested their hypothesis to maximize their efficiency:

Interviewer:    Do you ever say no to any of these requests?
Carol:          Sometimes I don't do them and see what happens [laughs]… I just think 'that is just going to use too much of my time and I don't think it's probably where my time is most valuably spent'.
Interviewer:    What does happen if you ignore some of these requests?
Carol:          Nothing usually [laughs], that's my experiment. I would like to be able to identify more accurately what is really valuable.

Yet there were times – and the non-senior managers were expert in identifying them – when requests could not be ignored. That did not mean, however, that they were complied with. Rob was programme leader for A levels, a first-tier manager role that divided his time equally between management duties and teaching. Rob's primary motivation in his role was the well-being and success of his students and it was this that he prioritized. What most interfered with this were the frequent and repetitive requests from senior managers for data. From Rob's perspective, these requests – which were considered endemic in the box-ticking culture of FE – meant taking time away from his real work. And so he *made out*: when he was asked for specific data, rather than spending his time searching through records and reports, he gave instinctive and estimated figures instead:

> If you look on that form there you'll see they've asked me about this data here. Now I could go back into the records and I could check that to make sure it's 100% accurate but I've given an

instinctive number. I could check that to make sure but I haven't
got the time to give them an absolute spot-on number [laughs].

Another example was provided by Elaine, a first-tier manager responsible
for managing access courses. As the college prepared for an impending
OFSTED inspection, senior managers were keen for curriculum leaders to
hold more team meetings to provide documentary evidence of accountability
and monitoring. Elaine felt that she and her team just didn't have the
time to hold even more meetings and so she fabricated the paperwork,
cobbling together impromptu conversations into a set of minutes. From her
perspective, the conversations were real, the work was real; she was just
re-presenting them as official meetings to avoid taking time from teaching
and learning.

These examples highlight the dialectical nature of non-senior
management within FE, the reality that sometimes managers have to resist
their own managers in order to do their jobs properly. At the heart of their
resistance is the proclivity to 'job-craft' (Wrzesniewski and Dutton, 2001),
a result of the socially constructed nature of work where individuals will
interpret their job in their own way, prioritizing those aspects that they find
personally meaningful and downplaying those aspects which are not. In this
way the FE managers resisted the formal delineation and specification of
their job in order to create a personalized role based upon their meaningful
purpose: senior managers imposed a role that concerned surveillance, human
resource procedures and control; the non-senior managers saw their role as
supporting students to succeed. As such, their resistance re-appropriates the
concept of management from the official definition, re-appropriates their
identity as teacher and manager, and re-appropriates time to spend on what
they consider to be more worthwhile work. In essence, they do the job as
they see it should be done.

Key to this resistant job-crafting was a final form of resistance:
resistance by distance created a values-based dis-identification with senior
managers that involves 'an internal monologue that sardonically debunks
management initiatives while externally complying with them' (Fleming,
2005: 49). This was achieved firstly by cynicism, a form of ambiguous
accommodation in Prasad and Prasad's (1998) typology that presented
senior leaders as incompetent, financially obsessed, reactive and removed
from the realities of teaching:

> I find it a strange thing that you'd think that people who were
> running an education establishment would have an understanding
> of education but when you look at the make-up of [our] senior

management team … you've got an accountant, you've got someone who's come from business and you've got this, that and the other and an MIS [management information system] person. So they're looking at systems and they're looking at figures and they're looking at tracking, they're looking at delivering evidence all the way through and what they're not seeing is the teaching side and recognizing that the teaching side needs time thrown at it. (Sue)

Cynicism made performing unsavoury managerial tasks more palatable but it also made resistant job-crafting less dissonant – if we distance ourselves cognitively from senior managers we feel less of an obligation to do as we are told. While Fleming and Spicer (2003: 162) consider cynicism as offering a 'specious sense of freedom', for managers in FE cynicism offers a sense of autonomy in how they perform their role and there is nothing specious about that.

Yet non-senior managers do not only resist as a means of re-appropriating professional autonomy, they also collude with the resistance of their teams, the teachers they line-manage. At one level, non-senior managers would collude with staff resistance via peripheral engagement with the 'piss-taking' of their teams, often aimed against senior college leaders, even in team meetings. A prime example is offered by Keith's chairing of his carpentry team meeting:

| | |
|---|---|
| Keith: | [Head of department] has asked us to make a retirement present for the principal – any suggestions? |
| Lecturer 3: | What do you call that wooden frame that has a length of rope hanging from it? |
| Lecturer 2: | Give him a picture of [the college] and say 'you arranged for this shit hole to be built'. |
| Keith: | What about a picture of us showing our arses? |
| Lecturer 2: | Give him one of the tree seats that have gone wrong – it'll remind him of this place. |

In other examples, managers would turn a blind eye to hard-working lecturers leaving early or arriving late, even giving covert permission for days off for events such as funerals when following procedures was onerous and time-consuming. But for non-senior managers, the resistance of their teams presented a dilemma: if they challenged resistance they risked being seen as identifying with senior managers and losing the cooperation of their teams; if they turned a blind eye they risked having their collusion discovered by senior managers and possible disciplinary action. Thus the managers adopted a situational approach to collusion and turning a blind eye when the resistance of their teams did not affect students, even joining in when it concerned mocking senior leaders or avoiding the complexity of college bureaucracy.

## Dancing unseen

Despite being formally designated as managers, for many first- and middle-tier managers in FE, resistance is a routine, everyday form of organizational behaviour. Yet resistance in FE is not purely an antagonistic reaction to subjugation by senior managers or a response to capitalist inequalities; colleges are not *real* capitalist organizations, despite the impact of marketization. Ultimately student success is the goal of colleges, rather than profit, however much that goal may become shrouded in the mists of fiscal discourse. Where resistance in private-sector organizations may be intentionally damaging to the goal of profit, the resistance of first-tier and middle managers is explicitly not intended to damage the goal of FE. In fact, resistance here has the exact opposite purpose – it is a means of prioritizing teaching and learning and student welfare at the expense of needless complexity and performativity. Resistance is a means of creating space: space within the working day and within processes and procedures, space that can be used for work of a far higher value. Resistance, then, is not solely a reaction to power, it is a form of academic citizenship that prioritizes students and teachers over the systemic reporting structures and financial imperatives upon which modern colleges are built. From this perspective, resistance is an ethical pursuit.

Care must also be taken that the resistance of non-senior managers is not reified as heroic – this is what a dialectic approach to the study of power and resistance seeks to avoid. In 'The Twelve Dancing Princesses', the soldier's resistance and collusion is not merely task-oriented, it creates space for self-interest – he gets to dance, watch the merriment and even drink. His resistance and collusion create space for personal satisfaction at work. While in FE there was little suggestion that managerial resistance was a facilitator of merriment, that does not mean that there was no element of self-interest. As much as resistance acted as a means of academic citizenship, it also allowed managers to avoid those tasks that they personally disliked or which would add to personal workloads or would cause conflict with their team, which they found stressful. In other cases it involved self-interest even more directly: in Kevin's college there was a policy that no one could take four weeks' continuous leave in the summer so he took one week off, came in for half a day then took three more weeks' leave. Thus, rather than being perceived as heroic, resistance should be seen above all as pragmatic, the cultivation of practices and behaviours that get things done and enhance personal job satisfaction.

One final question remains: how do managers get away with resisting? How do they dance unseen by either senior managers or the teams they manage? After all, in a sector dominated by managerialism, managers who are identified as resistant are unlikely to remain in post; similarly, lecturers who perceive their line-managers as highly resistant are likely to interpret this as a cue to resist, themselves. The detection of managerial resistance is therefore to be avoided and in this, first-tier and middle managers prove to be adept at walking the dialectic between compliance and resistance, managing and collusion. Two strategies facilitated this achievement: invisibility and impression management, the two strategies also employed by the soldier. Resistance was not routinely of the overt and visible kind – while there were instances of open confrontations with senior managers, the majority of non-senior managers were wily enough to avoid these. Ignoring requests, for example, was difficult to detect in organizations renowned for forgetfulness; working the system was almost impossible to detect because surveillance in colleges was founded upon systems being breached, not manipulated. The second strategy was to manage impressions by appearing to do what was being asked, in the way it was being asked, while in reality doing it in their own way. If data was requested and estimated data was given, there was often no way of senior managers noticing the difference; if spontaneous conversations were presented as official minutes, the impression was one of compliance. The ultimate means of remaining undetected, however, was achievement: it was increasing student success rates, improving attendance, raising lesson observation grades. When things were working, senior managers maintained their distance and pretence became more secure, invisibility easier. And it was ultimately this organizational focus on the ends rather than the means that allowed managers to dance.

## Conclusion

Without the soldier, the story of 'The Twelve Dancing Princesses' would act as a metaphor for traditional notions of power and resistance within organizations, a labour process theory picture of power and resistance where power ultimately wins. What the soldier adds is the micro-political, the dialectical complications, contradictions and tensions of organizational life, found in exemplary form within FE colleges and wonderfully enacted by first-tier and middle managers. Simultaneously manager and teacher, subjugator and subjugated, it is the very liminality of their position, the pull of competing forces and priorities that engenders resistance and collusion. Yet managerial resistance is difficult to pin down: it is a means to create space to get the job done properly; it is the re-appropriation of professional autonomy; it is a form of academic citizenship, yet it is also self-interested. In all its forms, for all its motivations, resistance allows managers to achieve the goal of student success in the best way they can because, while the dancing may be unseen, the danger of losing their head should they fail is very real.

## References

Burawoy, M. (1979) *Manufacturing Consent: Changes in the labor process under monopoly capitalism*. Chicago: University of Chicago Press.

Collinson, D. (2014) 'Dichotomies, dialectics and dilemmas: New directions for critical leadership studies?' *Leadership*, 10 (1), 36–55.

Fleming, P. (2005) 'Metaphors of resistance'. *Management Communication Quarterly*, 19 (1), 45–66.

Fleming, P., and Spicer, A. (2003) 'Working at a cynical distance: Implications for power, subjectivity and resistance'. *Organization*, 10 (1), 157–79.

Mumby, D.K. (2005) 'Theorizing resistance in organization studies: A dialectical approach'. *Management Communication Quarterly*, 19 (1), 19–44.

Prasad A., and Prasad, P. (1998) 'Everyday struggles at the workplace: The nature and implications of routine resistance in contemporary organizations'. *Research in the Sociology of Organizations*, 15 (2), 225–57.

Wrzesniewski, A., and Dutton, J. (2001) 'Crafting a job: Revisioning employees as active crafters of their work'. *Academy of Management Review*, 26 (2), 179–201.

'FE gave me the chance to become the person and dancer I want to be in life.'

James Furlong

*Chapter 10*

# Dancing in plain sight
*Doug Rouxel*

*'Jumping from boulder to boulder and never falling, with a heavy pack, is easier than it sounds; you just can't fall when you get into the rhythm of the dance.'*

(Jack Kerouac)

## Introduction

This chapter examines a number of recent disputes in the FE sector around the professional position of teachers, in particular the dispute over the compulsory payment of fees to the Institute for Learning (IfL). This represents a particularly good example of how the sector responded – like the princesses in the dance – by taking a stand that was about not only resistance but also about positive action. What was fascinating about the IfL dispute was not that people hated the fees – which they did – it was the related discussion about what it meant to be a teacher in FE. At its root this was a discussion about what FE is for. I argue that real change to FE must evolve from this kind of dialogue, not one about funding methodologies, the right key performance indicators, or what success rates are ideal in your subject area. Such dialogue is not even about which teaching approaches will ensure time to fulfil administrative duties alongside teaching. More important than any of these is rescuing the classroom from the statisticians and bean counters. Teachers need to reclaim the classroom and the whole sector, not for the fulfilment of numerical targets, but for the sake of meaningful education.

Dancing in plain sight involves taking opportunities like those offered by the online forums that cropped up around the IfL website at the time of the fees dispute. In these forums, discussion went significantly beyond the details of the dispute itself and into much more fundamental areas of teaching and learning, and the purpose of FE.

## Measuring education

Metrics and performance indicators have come to define the professional worth of teachers both inside and outside the FE sector, which contributes to an active erosion of teachers' professional identity. As abstract data becomes the principal lens through which their work is seen, so teachers are forced to focus less on education and more on providing 'correct' data (Ball, 2003). This reliance on the measurable has manifested itself in a general top-down and technocratic approach to education from college managers, sector bodies and the government. It has led to a crisis of professional identity among teachers in the sector, as notions of added value, efficiency and outputs have replaced the ethics, values and trust on which the shared identity of teachers was previously built. Resistance to diminished conceptions of the professional role of teachers in FE was a feature of the dispute over membership of the IfL.

The FE sector has seen several disputes that have arisen not from the traditional concerns of pay or terms and conditions, but from a threat to the professional position of teachers. One such dispute arose at Westminster Kingsway College in London where the local union branch operated a two-year boycott of teaching observations, opposing in particular the use of unannounced observations. These were perceived as a disciplinary tool rather than a means of addressing professional educational concerns.

Elsewhere, one of the most significant local disputes in recent times where professionalism and performance indicators were central was the so-called 'Halesowen 4' dispute, in early 2013. This dispute was sparked by the dismissal of four teachers from Halesowen College's mathematics department. The college's position was that these teachers were dismissed for failing to ensure that students fulfilled their potential and achieved their expected levels of attainment. The evidence the college used to support this judgement was almost exclusively built on comparing their students' A level examination results with college and national benchmarks. The regional union official accused the college of making selective use of the data in justifying their position, and argued that: 'There is now a question over whether teachers in FE colleges can be dismissed purely on students' attainment, making it a national issue' (quoted in Radford, 2013). The Halesowen 4 dispute arose directly from performance indicators representing the outcomes of an educational institution, department or individual teacher. It exposed the assumption that education is in some way quantifiable, and that teacher performance can thus be measured as providing either enough or insufficient learning. The notion of a surplus in this situation is never addressed.

A system where success is based on comparing course data with those of the average of a wider set, in which the original course is included, will mean that by this measure many courses are unsuccessful. There is, moreover, a tension between the complexity of the system by which FE teachers, departments and institutions are judged, as against the case that the outcomes on which performance indicators are based are often beyond the control of teachers, managers and even college principals. Expected standards are inconsistent and impossible for every course to meet. This system ensures that a large number of courses will be seen as failing, which can have a profound impact at the institutional level in terms of funding, and at an individual level as in Halesowen, where teachers might lose their jobs. The logic behind the way these comparative data are used is that the quality of the relationship with the teacher is the sole determinant in the student's achievement. This is not, however, the case. For example, students leave courses for a multitude of reasons (Yorke, 1999) that do not necessarily imply that the course, the college or the teaching is of poor quality.

Intrinsic to this system of surveillance are financial imperatives that are crucial to any explanation of the erosion of teachers' professionalism in FE. If the use of metrics leads to behaviour that is against the pedagogic interests of the community in which a college serves, 'the money helps to persuade you that it's a good idea', as an FE college manager said (quoted in Smith, 2007: 59), adding that 'colleges saw the bottom line of their accounts and put that in front of the education of students'. This kind of unethical behaviour that derives from the culture of audit within the FE sector is a demonstration of how certain performance indicators may impact on the professionalism of FE teachers. What Ball (2003) has termed the 'reprofessionalization' of teachers is marked by the co-option of the professional identity of FE teachers into the marketization agenda. This places competition and the possibility of performing better than your peers at the centre of the professional identity. As the disputes at Halesowen and Kingsway colleges demonstrate, however, there has been resistance to some of these moves and the professional role of FE teachers has been a distinct area of contention in the conflict between pedagogical and other imperatives.

The most prominent dispute involving the professional standing of FE teachers centred on charging fees directly to all members of the IfL. Formed in 2002, the IfL started as a voluntary membership-led body to represent the professional interests of FE teachers. This position altered significantly with the implementation of The Further Education Teachers' Continuing Professional Development and Registration (England) Regulations in 2007, which introduced the statutory requirement to belong to the IfL in order to gain and maintain a licence to practise as a teacher in the sector. These regulations also included the requirement to undertake at least 30 hours of continuing professional development (CPD) per year, which also was to be monitored and enforced by the IfL.

When membership of the IfL had first become a statutory requirement the government paid the membership fees. In the period following the implementation of the new regulations few FE teachers were openly hostile to the IfL, even if support for the organization was lukewarm. Then at the FE sector conferences of the main FE teachers' union, the University and College Union (UCU), in 2009 and 2010, motions were passed which noted concern about the IfL and which instructed the Further Education Committee of the union to review the operations of the IfL and report back to the conference. A mood of engagement with the IfL nonetheless prevailed in these debates. Until this point, many teachers' only contact with the IfL had been when they were expected to report the CPD that they had undertaken to the organization, as the responsible body, generally in a crude account of the number of hours. Though this was a rather reductive measure of professionalism, the IfL was involved with many other developmental activities and almost certainly had some positive influences on the sector. However, these were not always apparent to teachers whose relationship with the IfL was mediated principally through the mechanistic reporting of CPD hours.

The period of mild indifference towards the IfL came to an abrupt end immediately the funding of membership fees from central government ceased. At that point all FE teachers were expected to pay the organization directly to maintain their membership and so their licence to practise. The announcement of this proposal was met with widespread opposition and the beginning of a serious backlash against the IfL. It led to arguably the most widely supported industrial action seen in the FE sector since the incorporation of colleges in 1993. This backlash against the IfL can be tracked across the UCU's FE sector conference in 2011, which passed motions instructing the union to lead a collective boycott of the IfL, and in 2012 where a motion was passed condemning the IfL for its failures, and congratulating members for taking part in the collective boycott of payment of the IfL's membership fees.

The exact numbers involved in the boycott are difficult to ascertain because figures for non-renewal of membership were not published at the time. Based on the number of teachers in the broader lifelong sector who were potential members and the number that had actually renewed their membership by July 2011 as outlined by the IfL to the *Times Educational Supplement,* it appears that more than 130,000 teachers refused to pay. This is well in excess of the 34,505 FE members of UCU at the time of the formal industrial action ballot over the fees boycott.

On first glance this dispute might be interpreted as simply being about opposition to a charge of £68 per year (later reduced to £38 in response to sectoral opposition to the fee) to, in effect, have the right to carry on working. Through the course of the campaign, however, it became apparent that there was more to the dispute than that. The IfL dispute encapsulated concerns not just about payment to receive a service that many FE teachers did not recognize, let alone value, but other concerns about the expectations of them as professionals. The anti-fees campaign became a lightning rod for more fundamental opposition to the direction FE had been taken by the government. The campaign against fees also involved opposition to the government's target-led approach, both to the funding methodology and to the assessment of the quality of provision. Though well beyond the direct responsibility of the organization, the IfL found itself confronting general dissatisfaction with the priorities and management of FE.

In addition to being in the wrong place at the wrong time, the IfL's leadership tended towards a contradictory approach to dealing with members. It consistently described itself as member-led, yet throughout the fees dispute its official response was dismissive of legitimate concerns raised by members. In an interview in 2011 in *FE Week*, the IfL's Chief Executive suggested that some of the backlash against the IfL was offensive and hurtful, but the organization was at the same time unresponsive to constructive criticism. Similarly, when asked by *The Guardian* about a petition against the fees, the IfL's leadership's response was to question the legitimacy of the petition rather than engage with the concerns it raised. This dismissive approach led to even more animosity between the IfL's members and the organization.

Significantly, the dispute was driven not from the top of the trade union but from below, from union members and non-members alike who were committed to opposing payment of the IfL's fees. These people took to social media to discuss their reasons for condemning the IfL and to complain about the deprofessionalization of their roles, the redundancies in FE colleges and the reductive performance indicators that dominated management practice in the sector. The IfL had always had a significant social media presence; its Deputy Chief Executive was particularly active on Twitter and often engaged in discussions on Facebook and LinkedIn. As the boycott gained support and members or would-be members asked more questions of the IfL, the organization's formal presence on social media shrank and it started to block out opposition voices. It restricted posting on once open Facebook groups and limited membership of its LinkedIn community, so that far from being led by its membership, the IfL was increasingly restricting and policing what the membership wished to express online.

Although the dispute was at points acrimonious, the online spaces that opened up for discussion about the nature of FE were both interesting and inspiring for those involved. Discussions about what FE was for, as well as the nature of teachers' professional identity, took place in staffrooms and corridors, but also online through social media. Social media groups where the most energetic campaigners discussed these issues also helped spread support for the vote to boycott fees in the formal union ballot for industrial action, which came well after many people had started withholding the fees themselves. These online groups ensured that individuals isolated in their institution could also get involved in the wider discussions that arose from the dispute. In other words, the dispute opened up a space in which to examine what professionalism meant.

We see that the pervasive culture within FE, undermining the autonomy and professionalism of FE teachers, has met with resistance. The disputes outlined here are high-profile examples. The use of industrial action in its widest sense can be effective in this resistance, with the IfL dispute in particular precipitating a significant amount of discussion, review and, finally, change in government policy. As Robson (1998) has highlighted and as the anti-fees campaign argued, however, much change in FE is instigated from outside colleges, and especially by central government. This means that, while resistance to the deprofessionalization of teachers must come from within the sector, fundamental change is unlikely to be achieved solely from within it. Using the metaphor of the princesses, it was the soldier – the outsider – who was the catalyst that moved the story along. Other dangers exist. If we fail to resist the pressures of funding on the basis of performance indicators, and we see pay becoming related to the same performance indicators, then it seems highly likely that prospects for continuing employment will sooner or later be linked directly to them as well.

Those who wish to see real progress in FE, and teachers who are able to meet the needs of diverse students, have to put pressure on government to reverse policies that have reduced the educational process to a set of crude numerical values. There is a need for a more widespread resistance against the audit culture found in the sector because it has permeated the everyday lives of teachers and has had a profound impact on what it means to be a professional in FE. Plowright and Barr (2012) outline a vision of FE teacher professionalism that has ethical behaviour as a central pillar and where values are intrinsic to both personal and corporate behaviours. This inspiring vision recognizes above all that the judgements made in order to manage student–teacher relationships in a supportive and sensitive way are the expression of true FE professionalism.

## Postscript

As the final draft of this was being written, the Non-Executive Board of the IfL recommended to its Advisory Council that the IfL close and the legacy assets be passed to the newly founded Education and Training Foundation (ETF) through a deed of gift. This entailed the end of the IfL and potentially the opening of a new chapter in the battle over the professional identity of FE teachers. The closure of IfL may yet spark a more coherent discussion about a progressive professional identity of FE teachers, but we will have to wait and see if this changes the context of the dance.

## References

Ball, S. (2003) 'The teacher's soul and the terrors of performativity'. *Journal of Education Policy*, 18 (2), 215–28.

Plowright, D., and Barr, G. (2012) 'An integrated professionalism in further education: A time for phronesis?' *Journal of Further and Higher Education*, 36 (1), 1–16.

Radford, E. (2013) 'Union strike threat over new dismissals'. Online. http://tinyurl.com/bc462tj (accessed 10 October 2014).

Robson, J. (1998) 'A profession in crisis: Status, culture and identity in the further education college'. *Journal of Vocational Education and Training*, 50 (4), 585–607.

Smith, R. (2007) 'Of "duckers and divers", mice and men: The impact of market fundamentalism in FE colleges post-incorporation'. *Research in Post-Compulsory Education*, 12 (1), 53–69.

Yorke, M. (1999) *Leaving Early: Undergraduate non-completion in higher education*. London: Falmer Press.

'FE has widened my perspective in life, giving me personal fulfilment and opening up another pathway in my journey.'

Pei Tong

*Chapter 11*

# Action for ESOL: Pedagogy, professionalism and politics
*Rob Peutrell*

> '*Lermontov: When we first met … you asked me a question to which I gave a stupid answer, you asked me whether I wanted to live and I said "Yes". Actually, Miss Page, I want more, much more. I want to create, to make something big out of something little – to make a great dancer out of you. But first, I must ask you the same question, what do you want from life? To live?*
> *Vicky: To dance.*'

(Michael Powell and Emeric Pressburger)

## Introduction

This chapter explores a recent example of democratic, activist professionalism among FE teachers, the Action for ESOL campaign. Action for ESOL was launched in January 2011 following the announcement in November 2010 that the Coalition Government planned major cuts in funding for English for Speakers of Other Languages (ESOL) for the following academic year. Its success in challenging government policy made the campaign unique in the recent history of FE. It was unique also in the ways in which it linked the issue of educational provision explicitly to those of teacher professionalism, pedagogy and politics.

From the outset, the campaign was led by grassroots practitioners – teachers, researchers and curriculum managers. It was supported by the lecturer's union, UCU (University and College Union), of which many participants were members, but, importantly, the campaign retained its autonomy. It actively involved students and forged alliances with organizations outside education. The campaign was concerned with teachers' jobs, but its emphasis was on the value of publicly funded English-language provision and on the effects of withdrawing that provision from migrants and minority-language communities. Although the campaign was rooted in the particular culture and political context of ESOL, its experience has wider relevance to the debates and struggles within contemporary FE.

I begin by placing Action for ESOL in its policy and political context and by identifying the policy and ideological drivers that led to the campaign.

I look at the campaign itself, showing how ESOL teachers (to borrow from C. Wright Mills) sought to transform the troubles of their particular milieu into a public issue. Following this, I discuss the ESOL Manifesto, a collectively produced statement of beliefs and values that emerged from the campaign, drawing detailed attention to its key themes. Finally, I consider the relevance of Action for ESOL for the struggles of other teachers in FE, to protect educational provision and to reimagine what it means to be a professional educator.

## The context

In November 2010, the Coalition Government's Department for Business, Innovation and Skills published its strategy document for FE, *Investing in Skills for Sustainable Growth* (BIS, 2010), in which they outlined their intention to make large-scale cuts in ESOL funding. From September 2011, only ESOL students from 'settled communities' actively seeking work and on the so-called 'active benefits' of Jobseeker's Allowance or work-related Employment Support Allowance would be entitled to full fee remission. Other changes included a reduction in the funding rate for ESOL programmes and the end of funding for workplace ESOL.

The implications of the proposed changes were unprecedented, the National Association for Teachers of English and Community Language to Adults (NATECLA) describing them in their response to BIS as 'the most serious crisis for the future of ESOL that has ever been seen'. The Association of Colleges (AoC) calculated that some 75 per cent of ESOL students would no longer be entitled to free English classes but instead would be expected to pay between £400 and £1,200. The effects would be felt particularly by women, who accounted for three-quarters of ESOL students on inactive benefits such as income support. In addition, asylum seekers would be excluded from the new provisions because they were prevented by law from seeking work so were not entitled to active benefit. The ambiguous notion of settled communities also sounded alarm bells for the ability of low-waged migrant workers to access ESOL courses. Ending funding for work-based ESOL suggested that migrant workers were not regarded as settled. Unlike members of longer-standing communities, they would no longer qualify for fee remission through claiming benefits such as working tax credit or housing benefit.

ESOL teachers were at a loss to understand how the proposed cuts were consistent either with the widely accepted view that English language skills were crucial to integration in a practical sense, or with the consensus among mainstream politicians that migrants had an obligation to learn English. If, as Sheila Rosenburg observed, ESOL had been 'positioned at the centre of government concern over social cohesion, identity and national security' (2007: 261), cuts of this scale made little sense at all. Rather, as NATECLA stated in response to the proposals, they would 'jeopardise all the work that [had] been built up over the years in producing good quality and well-resourced provision and a trained workforce'.

It was not that policy makers were unaware of the benefits of ESOL. For instance, there was a well-established correlation between poor English language skills, unemployment, low-skill employment and low wages (Carr-Hill *et al.*, 1996). Under the refugee integration strategy of the previous Labour Government, knowledge of English was regarded as essential for enabling refugees to find work, access public services and participate actively as citizens (Ager and Strang, 2004). Indeed, in the absence of a broader strategy for the integration of migrants as a whole, it was suggested that ESOL had been the principal means for achieving that end, albeit 'through increased demand rather than strategic intention' (Spencer, 2011: 217).

The inconsistency of policy was an obvious weak point in the coalition proposals. In a briefing posted on its website in February 2011, Action for ESOL expressed the views of many ESOL practitioners that English-language education made a vital contribution to integration and that the hidden costs of reducing funding had not been taken into account. It argued that:

> Reducing or marginalising ESOL provision is a false economy. Investment in ESOL *reduces* the need for spending in other areas, such as interpreting, translating and welfare benefits. ESOL is the most cost-effective way of drawing new arrivals and longer-term residents into local communities and enabling them to contribute to the economy and society as a whole.
>
> (Action for ESOL, 2011: n.p.)

If the cuts in provision were inconsistent with the practical benefits of ESOL, they were also seen as incongruous given the ideological perspective on English language learning that had emerged over the preceding years. To a large extent, this perspective was rooted in the discourse of community cohesion that emerged from the Labour Government's response to the disturbances in Oldham and other northern cities in 2001. Unrest in these cities was considered to be the result of communities living 'parallel lives' (Home Office, 2001), a view shared by many politicians and commentators of the centre-left and right, for whom multiculturalism had undermined solidarity and the idea of common citizenship (see, for example, Goodhart, 2004; Phillips, 2002; Putnam, 2007).

The London bombings of 2005 and Islamic radicalization added urgency to this perspective. Knowledge of English was posited as a precondition of citizenship and shared national identity, and migrants were often positioned as responsible for the apparent breakdown of community relations because of their perceived lack of interest in learning the language. Ironically, some months after the announcement of the cuts to ESOL funding, Prime Minster David Cameron reiterated the demand that migrants learn English, arguing that the inability of some migrants to the UK to speak English contributed to a sense of 'discomfort and disjointedness in some neighbourhoods' (Cameron, 2011). Lack of English was also viewed as a cause of tensions within minority communities.

A decade before Cameron's speech, Home Secretary David Blunkett (2002) had argued that by not speaking English at home, Asian families contributed to an intergenerational 'schizophrenia' within their communities. Yet, perhaps more than any other event, it had been the introduction of language and citizenship tests for migrants seeking naturalization following the Nationality, Immigration and Asylum Act 2002 that most clearly expressed the view that speaking English was a fundamental requisite of citizenship. While language testing expressed the well-established symbolic role of a national language in the ideology of the nation-state (and language testing is by no means unique to the UK (Shohamy and McNamara, 2009)), it again highlighted the crucial role of ESOL in the migrant transition to citizenship.

If language has symbolic meaning, it follows that attitudes towards language always encode cultural and political values (Cameron, 1995). Arguments about English are also arguments about the status of minority languages and the people who speak them (Blackledge, 2009; Cameron, 2013). Requiring migrants to learn English revealed views about both the nature of UK society and the perceived threats of migration, multiculturalism and multilingualism to its integrity and future, and was a means of imposing linguistic and cultural uniformity on an increasingly pluralistic society (Blackledge, 2009). The consequent stigmatization of minority languages and minority-language speakers provided an important fillip to the campaign; the claim that migrants were uninterested in learning English was recognized as simply wrong.

This argument persists, however, despite the evidence that the supply of language classes has never been sufficient to meet demand (Bloch, 2002; Phillimore *et al.*, 2007; Davies, 2013). Indeed, House of Commons library research suggested that ESOL had been 'a victim of its own success' under the previous Labour Government, as unpredicted demand resulted in rising expenditure on ESOL (Hubble and Kennedy, 2011). The costs of meeting the demand for ESOL classes had been the subject of an inquiry into ESOL funding and provision by the National Institute for Adult and Continuing Education (NIACE, 2006). In 2007, increasing expenditure was used to justify the removal of automatic fee remission for ESOL students and restrictions on the rights of asylum seekers to enrol on ESOL programmes. Despite its popularity, these measures clearly demonstrated the vulnerability of ESOL to political pressure, and were an indication of things to come. The cuts in 2007 too had resulted in a national campaign involving ESOL teachers, the Defend ESOL campaign.

## The campaign

The Action for ESOL campaign launched in January 2011 was followed by eight months of intense work by teachers, researchers, students and members of refugee and migrant welfare and rights groups, until the government announced a near U-turn just as the new academic year was due to start.

Over this time, the campaign made use of many of the tactics associated with radical social movements: a national petition; letter writing; briefings; rallies, demonstrations and lobbies; local and national alliance building; gaining the support of sympathetic politicians and councillors and the endorsement of public figures, trade unions and civic organizations; producing local impact studies; arranging radio and television interviews; and making use of the range of social media, including practitioner e-bulletins. It was urgent, but it was also celebratory and, at times, carnivalesque. Events included picnics, teach-ins, silent protests, noisy protests and giving out food. A national Day of Action on 23 March saw rallies and other events in cities such as Bradford, Bristol, Leeds, Halifax and Nottingham and a march of hundreds of teachers and students to Downing Street, where the national petition was delivered to the Prime Minister.

Calling ALL Students!

# Make a Noise for ESOL!

## Thursday 19th May at 12.15 and/or 1pm
### Come out and shout your support for ESOL!

From September the government will cut much ESOL funding. Over 50% of ESOL students will not be able to return to college. Show your support for them and make as much noise as possible at 12.15 or 1pm with other groups of students and teachers. Bring instruments, pots, pans, clap your hands or just shout!
Together we can make a difference

For more campaigning ideas:
www.actionforesol.org.uk

Make a Noise for ESOL – one of many flyers produced during the campaign. Humour and a lively public presence were important in raising awareness of ESOL

ESOL students pose outside Parliament. Covered mouths draw attention to the consequences of the proposed ESOL cuts on people with limited English – exclusion and silencing

Among the many posts and images on the Action for ESOL website and Facebook page, one example posted by teachers in Halifax following the Day of Action captures the enthusiasm that defined the campaign:

> Brilliant day at Parkinson Lane School in Halifax yesterday. WEA learners made samosas and handed them out, with publicity leaflets to members of the public and parents at the end of the school day. Chaotic and noisy with lots of signing and chanting – all with the support of the wonderful headteacher there.

From the start, the campaign actively involved students as participants – marching, banner making and letter writing. Students wrote and spoke eloquently and often publicly about the value of their ESOL classes, giving interviews, speaking at rallies and appearing on videos uploaded to YouTube. Their message was clear: they wanted to learn English and for many, funding cuts and further restrictions on fee remission would make this impossible. Many teachers used class time to help students to get their message out, by writing letters and testimonials. Materials on the effects of the cuts were produced for use in class and shared via social media. In this way, language learning was linked to real events affecting the lives of ESOL students and a real struggle outside the classroom, the campaign providing an opportunity for creative, critical pedagogy. In one case, a group of ESOL students learned the skills of film-making to produce a video report of the Day of Action in London that was uploaded to YouTube.

The campaign worked closely with the Refugee Council, Migrants Rights Network and NIACE, contributing to its parliamentary briefing event in March 2011. In addition, the campaign maintained links with the AoC, itself busy lobbying ministers and civil servants with information provided by its member colleges, through the UCU national officer for FE, Dan Taubman.

Surprisingly, not all college managers were supportive of the campaign. Activists reported indifference and even hostility from some college managers, and, it must be said, from some ESOL teachers. It was reported that one local authority even threatened ESOL tutors with dismissal if they took part in protests or spoke to the media about funding cuts (Webber, 2011). Campaigning publicly for the rights of ESOL students was not without controversy; the contested nature of teacher professionalism was evident in the contrasting attitudes found among both college managements and practitioners.

In late August 2011, the government changed its mind. The crucial issue of fee remission for students not on 'active benefit' had been won. *The Guardian* reported that the U-turn was made with 'no big announcement; the news slipped out quietly via funding guidance documents published on the Skills Funding Agency's website' (Murray, 2011). Many argued that the change in policy did not go far enough. Fees were still an obstacle for many students not in receipt of a qualifying benefit, while the funding rate for ESOL was still reduced. Yet, although colleges anticipating huge reductions in student enrolments were thrown into chaos, ESOL teachers and students had good cause to celebrate. The success of the campaign was a rare event in today's FE sector.

## The ESOL Manifesto

Perhaps one of the most distinctive features of the campaign was the collective production of the *ESOL Manifesto* (Action for ESOL, 2012), a statement of the campaign's beliefs, values and demands. Between 80 and 100 teachers and others contributed to the discussion and the subsequent drafting of the final text. The vision of teacher professionalism articulated in the manifesto was democratic and activist, one that refused to be restricted to compliance with institutional and policy mandates. Its vision was exemplified by the participatory way in which the manifesto was written. Inevitably, there was much that participants agreed on. But consensus was achieved despite differences of opinion, including whether government policy on language and citizenship should be described as racist, whether language education was a right, and what attitude the campaign should take to small businesses that recruited low-waged migrant workers.

The manifesto began with a national seminar organized at the UCU offices in London, in June 2011, Defending Our Practice and Profession: Where we've come from, where we are now and where we're going. Following short presentations, the 60 or so participants were asked to reflect on the past, present and possible futures for ESOL and in discussion groups agree themes and statements to be carried forward into the manifesto. These themes were the basis of the first draft of the manifesto, which, together with a copy of the notes, was circulated to seminar participants by email and made available to others through the Action for ESOL website and Facebook page, the NATECLA website and the ESOL-Research Network e-list.

A second seminar was arranged for early September, shortly after the U-turn had been announced. The notice advertising the seminar stressed that the aim of the manifesto was to 'mobilise the ESOL community and its supporters in defence of language education' and 'promote discussion within the ESOL community in regard to provision, pedagogy and professionalism'. Reference was made not only to challenging the government in regard to funding, but also the ESOL profession itself in terms of its 'pedagogic ethos and political responsibilities'. At this seminar, the draft manifesto was discussed in detail, with changes agreed to both content and language. After further redrafting by a small group of volunteers, the text was re-circulated through social media. Discussion and revision continued into January, almost up to the moment it was prepared for printing and uploading onto the Action for ESOL website. The manifesto was formally launched on 3 March 2014 at the UCU office. Guest speakers included UCU President, Kathy Taylor, and Heidi Alexander, one of a small number of Labour MPs who had actively supported the campaign.

The manifesto opens by recognizing that, while the government had retreated on the most significant changes announced in November 2010, ESOL remained vulnerable to 'the whims of policy makers and funders' (Action for ESOL, 2012: 2). To better resist these in the future, it argues that teachers need:

> [...] a strong collective identity, a clear sense of the purpose of ESOL and confidence in ourselves as qualified, knowledgeable, committed professionals.
>
> (ibid.: 3)

The manifesto recognizes that ESOL is a diverse sector and that not all ESOL teachers will agree with the views expressed in it. Nonetheless, its argument is clear; ideas and debate are crucial if teachers are to have any say in shaping the future of ESOL provision.

The seven sections of the manifesto reflect the range of issues that emerged through the campaign and seminars: Defending our Sector; Funding; Language, Community and Diversity; Defending the ESOL Identity; Professionalism; and Pedagogy. Taken together, these headings convey an understanding of teacher professionalism that is both political and pedagogic, and this is evident in what I consider to be the manifesto's three key themes.

It was crucial for students to have a voice in the campaign – as speakers and writers. This powerful, somewhat iconic, image was used to illustrate the cover of the manifesto

First, the manifesto contests policy at the ideological level. It argues that language education is a 'public good which contributes to society as a whole' but more controversially that 'the opportunity to learn the common language of the community in which you live and work is a human right' (ibid.: 4). Thus, while recognizing the importance of English language for social participation, the manifesto challenges the one-sided interpretation of language learning as an obligation on migrants. Rather, it stresses the responsibility of the state to provide effective opportunities for learning

English for all those living and working in the UK, regardless of their formal status.

In addition, the manifesto argues that the right to language education is 'inseparable from the right to cultural and linguistic identity' (ibid.: 5). Thus it contests the prevailing antipathy towards multiculturalism and multilingualism and the racialized immigration and cultural agenda in which language is used as a 'proxy for race' (ibid. 5). Equally, it recognizes that ESOL students are diverse – linguistically, culturally, socially and in their reasons for learning English. Crucially, language education and language rights are seen as a matter of enabling non-native English speakers 'to have a voice and live autonomous fulfilling lives, in community with others' (ibid.: 5).

Second, the manifesto contests policy in terms of provision and pedagogy. It argues that ESOL provision should be 'accessible, comprehensive and integrated', reach out into the community and enable progression, to vocational and academic courses (ibid.: 6). The manifesto thus addresses the historically marginal status of ESOL within FE and the often fragmentary nature of language education, in which the community is disconnected from the mainstream, and ESOL provision discrete from vocational and academic programmes. Again, the manifesto emphasizes the 'autonomy of individual language students' and that provision should reflect *their* needs, circumstances and aspirations (ibid.: 7). Yet, if it is vital to defend and extend provision, the nature of that provision also matters.

Thus, while the manifesto recognizes the value of the Adult ESOL Curriculum and of examinations, it does so critically. It takes issue with what it perceives to be an over-centralized and inflexible approach that inadequately accommodates the diversity of student needs, while favouring the learning of 'skills' over meaning and encouraging institutions to value examinations because they generate funding rather than for their intrinsic benefits. In addition, the manifesto proposes a participatory and collaborative approach to the curriculum and that attention should be given to helping students develop the skills and aptitudes required for active, democratic citizenship. Reprising the tradition of critical and community adult education, the manifesto states that language education should concern:

> [...] the whole person. It is about the capacity of everyone – teachers and students alike – to take charge of our lives individually and collectively, and to participate actively and critically in all aspects of our world, in the classroom as well as beyond.
>
> (ibid.: 9)

Finally, the manifesto addresses the contested meaning of teacher professionalism. It maintains that the responsibilities of teachers go beyond what Kerry Kennedy (2005) has called the 'educational private sphere' of classroom practice and that 'to be truly professional', ESOL teachers have to engage with not only issues of the classroom but also with the social, cultural and political contexts within which language learning and the lives of language learners are embedded (ibid.: 7). As with all education, it argues, ESOL is shaped by power and culture. It follows that as educators and as democratic citizens, teachers have 'both a right and a responsibility' to engage in political and policy issues and debates that affect them and their students (ibid.: 7).

## The wider relevance of Action for ESOL

Despite what was at stake for its participants, the campaign was an energizing opportunity for learning, sharing and alliance building. However, a key question remains: is the experience of Action for ESOL of wider relevance to other teachers in FE? I think the answer is yes, provisionally. Its argument for a democratic, activist practice and identity is certainly relevant. Through the campaign, teachers defined their own sense of what being an educator means and demonstrated what could be achieved when teachers exercise their own collective agency.

This did not and could not mean that the tensions and struggles inherent in actual teaching work were resolved; far from it. Colleges and classrooms are messy and fraught with ideological and ethical dilemmas. Like other social actors, ESOL teachers have to work against prevailing discourses, finding opportunities for critical practice where they can in a spirit of 'principled pragmatism' (Cooke and Simpson, 2008: 45). Inevitably, critical awareness creates its own challenges and discomforts, not least a deepened sense of the gap between teachers' own values and those that suffuse the institutions and system within which they work. An activist network outside the formal institutional structures, such as Action for ESOL, at least provides a space and reference point that validates and empowers a different understanding of both education and professionalism.

Yet it would be wrong to claim that the experience of Action for ESOL is neatly applicable to other areas of the FE curriculum. FE comprises diverse 'learning cultures' (James and Biesta, 2007), while the different educational and occupational backgrounds and routes into teaching result in a 'rather fractured professional base' (Jephcote and Salisbury, 2009: 971) within the sector. Unlike some other areas of the curriculum, ESOL does not have a strong vocational identity which allies it with business ideologies and practices. Perhaps its traditionally marginal status allows a degree of independence denied to other subjects. Today, I suspect that ESOL is welcomed in FE because it brings funding, rather than out of a genuine interest in the pedagogy and purpose of language provision for migrant and minority-language communities. At the same time, ESOL retains a strong independent professional voice through NATECLA, an organization of around 500 teachers and researchers. NATECLA is a source of comment and lobbying on matters of concern to ESOL teachers, and an important link between research and practice. Similarly, the electronic ESOL Research List has over 850 subscribers, including ESOL teachers, researchers and administrators. This too provides an important forum for discussion of policy and practice, with its bulletins circulated more widely among non-subscribers. Like the Action for ESOL network itself, these networks will continue to provide a vital means of communication and mobilization into the future as ESOL faces new challenges.

ESOL is also embedded in a highly contested political space, and is, as Melanie Cooke (2011) has argued, political by nature. Issues of migration, race, cultural identity and citizenship are intrinsic to the field. The interpretation of these issues in policy has implications for funding and provision, and so for teachers' jobs and future prospects. This is not to deny that other areas of the curriculum are similarly politically and culturally embedded. Nonetheless, the political dimensions of language education are often pressing and overt, such that the interconnections between ESOL and the wider civic and activist worlds are more immediately obvious. The threat to ESOL funding provided a basis for collaboration between ESOL practitioners and refugee and migrant organizations not directly associated with education. What mattered was that activists in the campaign had the political imagination to recognize and act on these shared concerns.

However, the key message of the campaign was that grassroots teachers have not only the right but also the responsibility to engage politically in education. Although ethical and political choices are inherent in any educational setting, this expanded idea of what it means to be a professional educator is a challenge to teachers. As Freire (1972) pointed out, education can be either a means of perpetuating existing social relations or of developing the skills, values and dispositions needed to challenge and transform them. This raises crucial questions of teachers' identity, responsibility and accountability.

An ESOL student carries a UCU placard on the Day of Action, 23 March 2011. Action for ESOL believed that teachers should use their resources to enable students to participate in a common campaign

As teachers, we may be 'in the system', but our responsibility and accountability to our students, communities and profession means that we are often pitched 'against the system' too. As earlier activists argued, if professional workers such as teachers are to achieve social change in a context of crisis and austerity, we need to act politically in alliance with others, but especially with those who make use of the services we provide (London Edinburgh Weekend Return Group, 1980). Action for ESOL demonstrated how an activist, democratic professionalism was essential if provision, jobs and the rights of ESOL students were to be defended and alternative values to those of mainstream policy articulated.

## Final word

If we are to shift from the piecemeal defence of what exists to a more confident promotion of our own educational values, we need a sense of our own agency as teachers, rather than see ourselves as subject to the decisions of others. We should refuse the passivity of compliant professionalism, loosen institutional identities and create our own spaces for thought and action; following the central metaphor of this collection, we need spaces to dance in. The responsibility for claiming these spaces is ours; no one will make them for us. The Action for ESOL campaign was once such space.

## References

Action for ESOL (2011) untitled briefing. Online. http://tinyurl.com/kcqebvk (accessed 14 October 2014).

— (2012) *The ESOL Manifesto*. Online. http://tinyurl.com/nt33ybx (accessed 14 October 2014).

Ager, A., and Strang, A. (2004) *Indicators of Integration: Final report*. London: Home Office.

BIS (2010) *Investing in Skills for Sustainable Growth*. London: Department for Business, Innovation and Skills.

Blackledge, A. (2009) '"As a Country We Do Expect": The Further Extension of Language Testing Regimes in the United Kingdom'. *Language Assessment Quarterly*, 6 (1), 6–16.

Bloch, A. (2002) *Refugees' Opportunities and Barriers in Employment and Training*. Leeds: Corporate Document Services.

Blunkett, D. (2002) 'What does citizenship mean today?' *The Guardian*, 15 September. Online. http://tinyurl.com/p5f7xsm (accessed 6 February 2011).

Cameron, David (2011) 'David Cameron on immigration: full text of the speech'. *The Guardian*, 14 April. Online. http://tinyurl.com/qgp8xfg (accessed 16 May 2014).

Cameron, Deborah (1995) *Verbal Hygiene*. London: Routledge.

— (2013) 'The one, the many and the other: Representing multi- and mono-lingualism in post-9/11 verbal hygiene'. *Critical Multilingualism Studies*, 1 (2), 59–77.

Carr-Hill, R., Passingham, S., and Wolf, A. (1996) *Lost Opportunities: The language skills of linguistic minorities in England and Wales*. London: Basic Skills Agency.

Cooke, M. (2011) 'Politics, protests and pedagogy: Where next for ESOL?' *Language Issues*, 22 (2), 5–17.

Cooke, M., and Simpson, J. (2008) *ESOL: A critical guide*. Oxford: Oxford University Press.

Davies, E. (2013) 'Migrants want to learn English: Why isn't the government investing to help them do so?' *New Statesman,* 5 July. Online. http://tinyurl.com/q7hk8db (accessed 22 April 2014).

Freire, P. (1972) *Pedagogy of the Oppressed.* Harmondsworth: Penguin.

Goodhart, D. (2004) 'Too Diverse?' *Prospect*, February. Online. http://tinyurl.com/nn2n66j (accessed 10 February 2014).

Home Office (2001) *Community Cohesion: A Report of the Independent Review Team Chaired by Ted Cantle* (the Cantle Report). London: Home Office.

Hubble, S., and Kennedy, S. (2011) *Changes to funding for English for Speakers of Other Languages (ESOL) courses.* London: House of Commons Library Research Report. Online. www.parliament.uk/briefing-papers/SN05946.pdf (accessed 22 April 2014).

James, D., and Biesta, G. (2007) *Improving Learning Cultures in Further Education.* London: Routledge.

Jephcote, M., and Salisbury, J. (2009) 'Further education teachers' accounts of their professional identities'. *Teaching and Teacher Education*, 25, 966–72.

Kennedy, K. (2005) 'Rethinking Teachers' Professional Responsibilities: Towards a civic professionalism'. *International Journal of Citizenship and Teacher Education*, 1 (1), 3–15.

London Edinburgh Weekend Return Group (1980) *In and Against the State.* London: Pluto Press.

Murray, J. (2011) 'U-turn on ESOL funding causes enrolment mayhem for colleges'. *The Guardian*, 12 September. Online. http://tinyurl.com/oa3kspo (accessed 16 May 2014).

NIACE (2006) '*More than a language…': NIACE committee of inquiry on English for speakers of other languages. Final Report.* Leicester: NIACE.

Phillimore, J., Ergün, E., Goodson, L., and Hennessy, D. (2007) '"Now I do it by myself": Refugees and ESOL'. Birmingham: University of Birmingham Centre for Urban and Regional Studies and New Communities Network.

Phillips, M. (2002) 'The threat to national identity.' *Daily Mail*, 26 April. Online. www.melaniephillips.com/the-threat-to-national-identity (accessed 9 October 2014).

Putnam, R.D. (2007) 'E pluribus unum: Diversity and community in the twenty-first century'. The 2006 Johan Skytte Prize Lecture. *Scandinavian Political Studies*, 30 (2), 137–74.

Rosenburg, S. (2007) *A Critical History of ESOL in the UK: 1870–2006.* Leicester: NIACE.

Shohamy, E., and McNamara, T. (2009) 'Language assessment for immigration, citizenship, and asylum'. *Language Assessment Quarterly*, 6, 1–5.

Spencer, S. (2011) *The Migration Debate.* Bristol: The Policy Press.

Webber, F. (2011) 'Learn the language: How?' *Institute of Race Relations News Service*, 14 April. Online. www.irr.org.uk/news/learn-the-language-how/ (accessed 16 May 2014).

'FE has given me the tools I need for a career in a subject that I am passionate about, and fostered skills that I wasn't aware I had. The in-depth exploration of the subject gave me optimism about the future.'

Rowena Gander

# Chapter 12

# Beyond the metaphor:
# Time to take over the castle
*Rania Hafez*

> '*Dance in the middle of the fighting. Dance in your blood. Dance when you're perfectly free.*'

(Rumi)

It is telling that the metaphors we use to describe FE have come from fairy tales, and in the main involve oppressed princesses. We are either downtrodden Cinderella, the virtuous sister who toils selflessly day and night as a servant, or we are feisty princesses secretly defying our incarceration and having our moment on the dance floor. The escape into storytelling provides us with therapeutic release from the daily grind of the chalk face and the exigencies of management.

The fairytale similes, though largely accurate and justifiable, nevertheless expose our embarrassing impotence. Even when a metaphor offers an empowering representation of FE, as in the story of the dancing princesses, the seemingly positive allegory conceals the perennial problem for the sector's teachers and lecturers. Subversiveness may be what we do, but it is a dangerous and ultimately failed strategy. For it is in that very act of subversiveness that we concede the loss of what lies at the heart of being a professional: autonomy, authority and trust.

## 'Trust me, I am a teacher'

Professionalism may be a contested concept, but it has become the Holy Grail we FE lecturers claim we once possessed and we must regain. Perhaps we forget that professionalism in its historic manifestation was not a bestowed attribute, but an asserted one (Crook, 2008; McCulloch, 2011). What goes for being a professional nowadays is the antithesis of what it was to be a professional in times past. For, despite its 'slipperiness' (McCulloch, 2011), there are essential characteristics on which practitioners and writers have concurred: a profession is generally an autonomous, self-directed and self-managed association of experts.

In defining professionalism as such it is easy to see that it has been a while since FE teachers have been professional. There may be substance to the claim that they have been robbed of their professional status, but in seeking refuge in subversion, they are guilty of surrendering it.

Notwithstanding the inevitable evolution of professionalism as a social notion, the past three decades have seen a direct attack on the professionalism of FE teachers from several quarters. Political exigencies have joined with managerial ineptitude to undermine our authority and disciplinary expertise. But the more subtle and deeper undermining of FE teachers was not in the day-to-day operational control of their practice, but in the redefining of their contract with their public. Nowhere is that better articulated than in the speech by Estelle Morris, then New Labour's Secretary of State for Education. Speaking at the Social Market Foundation in 2001, she not only challenged the teaching profession to renew itself but questioned its fundamental claim to professional status:

> The professionalism must renew itself and restate its claim to pre-eminence. We are a long way from helping teaching to measure up to and surpass our ideals for what a profession can be. Teaching must remodel itself to keep up to date. Gone are the days when doctors and teachers could say, with a straight face, 'trust me, I'm a professional'. So we need to be clear about what does constitute professionalism for the modern world. And what will provide the basis for a fruitful and new era of trust between Government and the teaching profession.
>
> (Morris, 2001: 19)

In claiming that teachers had lost trust, the Secretary of State was laying a dangerous accusation against professionals and appointing government as the broker between them and the public. Teachers had to change and the parameters and extent of that change was to be defined by politicians, not by the professionals. This was an attack, not only on teachers' autonomy but also on the profession's own ability to define its scope. Now it was over to government to remodel teacher professionalism in a way that suited the political whims of the times.

The attack, although on teachers across all sectors, was particularly cutting when it came to teachers in FE. The 1993 reforms that saw the establishment of a quasi-market in the sector, through the incorporation of FE colleges, had led to a de facto exile of the FE teacher from the professional club. Around that time a new neighbour moved next door to me and I was delighted to find she was a teacher at a local school. 'I too am a teacher,' I declared proudly. 'Where do you teach?' asked my new neighbour. 'At the FE college,' I replied enthusiastically. 'Ah,' she said, making a face, 'you're not a real teacher then.' Then and now FE lecturers have been stranded in a professional wilderness, deemed to fall short of the virtuous school teachers, and lacking the academic credentials of university lecturers. This view has become more entrenched as skills rather than education became the policy and curriculum driver.

But politicians and fellow teachers were not alone in casting doubt over our professionalism. Writers on education had already identified emerging problems. As early as 1983 Donald Schön warned about the crisis of confidence in professional knowledge in the first chapter of his book *The Reflective Practitioner*. Schön charts the growth of the crisis through the erosion of teachers' self-confidence. He describes the loss of public confidence in the professions and the consequent questioning of their rights and freedoms. Professionals, he says, need to escape the morass of uncertainty, instability and value conflict that they face:

> The events which led from the triumphant professions of the early 1960s to the scepticism and unease of the 1970s and early 1980s have been at least as apparent to the professionals as to the general public. But the sense of confusion and unease which is discernible among leading professionals has an additional source. Professionals have been disturbed to find that they cannot account for processes they have come to see as central to professional competence.
>
> (Schön, 1983: 19)

Schön's point was that professionals cannot explain or justify, and therefore do not understand, what they are doing. So what Schön is identifying is a problem that arose in our own professional knowledge – our meta-cognition of what we do, how we do it, and more importantly why we do it. As a consequence professionals don't trust themselves and government doesn't trust professionals. This leads to a total erosion of our authority. Hence the next question that begs itself: how did we come to lose knowledge of our metier, and ourselves, and how do we regain it?

## Lost and found

We may have enjoyed a golden age once, particularly in the post-war era, when the notion of professionalism was exemplified by a teacher's independence and autonomy. Their teaching methodology, their relation to students and their judgements concerning assessment and examination were all their responsibility. The demarcation lines between government involvement and the profession's autonomy were famously drawn by George Tomlinson, Minister for Education, 1947–51. Blunt and working class (from the Bolton area), he made it clear that the government would not exercise direct control over the curriculum, allegedly declaring that 'Minister knows nowt about curriculum'.

Yet within a few years successive governments of all hues sought to exert increasing control over education. From Callaghan's Ruskin speech, which blamed teachers for slow economic development, to Thatcher's New Right schizophrenic policies, which curtailed local autonomy while strengthening central control, to Blair's Third Way, education and teachers increasingly became the focus of politicians' ire and at the same time the instrument of choice for social engineering. The legacy of this was an endless churn of policy initiatives leading to a morass of managerialist and bureaucratic practices in our colleges that stripped FE teachers of status and autonomy. And the tragedy of the situation is the tacit acceptance by teachers of that status. Sure, some of them do continue to subvert and sneak out and dance, but for the large majority, especially of new entrants to the profession, this is the only reality they know. It's not always the king standing guard at the locked door; most times it is fellow prisoners enforcing the curfew.

So how did we come to buy into our own incarceration? We cannot lay the blame solely on the politicians without recognizing the extent of contemporary seismic political change in society. What underlies the current crisis is a political and social shift in our attitude to knowledge. The recent past has witnessed a concerted attack on knowledge as a value and on education for its own sake (Young, 2012). As the social and economic aims of education replaced knowledge, it invariably led to the dismantling of teachers' authority and expertise, not least because of the teachers' own tacit acceptance of that loss. The authority that FE teachers have lost is one that emanates from their mastery of two key aspects of their work, epistemology and pedagogy – the supremacy of knowledge and the centrality of teaching. And we have lost both.

The attack on both knowledge and how we teach it has come in a much more dangerous way than technology and the internet. It is primarily social, and political. The social aspects of the erosion of both society's and teachers' authority was clearly articulated by Hannah Arendt in her seminal essay *The Crisis in Education*, first published in 1954. Arendt links authority to responsibility; in her case the responsibility of the educator is to represent the public wider world to students: 'The teacher's qualification consists in knowing the world and being able to instruct others about it, but his authority rests on his assumption of responsibility for that world' (Arendt, 1961: 189). It is that grounding in epistemology, expert knowledge of one's subject and discipline, coupled with pedagogy, the teacher's expertise in ushering the students into that knowledge, that gives teachers their authority.

The best way of understanding this is to look at a philosophical distinction between being **an** authority and being **in** authority. This was always a complex distinction and usually a professional was both **in** authority and **an** authority. There is now a complete separation between the two and FE teachers in particular are now seen and often are in authority without being an authority. The point of the distinction is epistemological. Being a professional and an authority meant that you had knowledge (and skills and perhaps a code of ethics) that justified your having a job and being seen by people as an authority to be taken on trust. An authority knows something – and that is the basis of trust.

We can't all know everything. Trust in the authority and knowledge of professionals makes possible a cultural milieu 'beyond the powers and capacities of any individual' (Bell, 1970: 194). In short, real empowerment of individual students does not come from endless directives on raising self-esteem and the centrality of the students' voice, but from investing trust in the authoritative knowledge of teachers. As Paulo Freire remarks in a lengthy exchange with Myles Horton:

> I also discovered another thing that was very important to me afterward, that I had authority but I was not authoritarian. I began to understand at a very young age that on one hand the teacher as a teacher is not the student. The student as the student is not the teacher. I began to perceive that they are different but not necessarily antagonistic. The difference is precisely that the teacher has to teach, to experience, to demonstrate authority and the student has to experience freedom in relation to the teacher's authority. I began to see that the authority of the teacher is absolutely necessary for the development of the freedom of the students.
>
> (Horton and Freire, 1990: 61)

In giving up this authority two new forms of professionalism have emerged: regulatory and therapeutic. The former is prescribed mainly by agents of government such as OFSTED and managers, and characterized by a demand for total uncritical compliance, and the latter is promoted by a social constructivist approach that has gone too far, reducing the teacher to a mere facilitator at best and a perpetual learner at worst, perpetually anxious, self-doubting and lacking in professional confidence.

The professional teacher–student relationship that Freire saw as empowering the student through the teacher's authority has been redefined as a therapeutic one. Therapy culture has replaced the culture of knowledge. At times the teacher is cast as the therapist, with the victim the student lacking in confidence, self-esteem, or only able to learn in one diminished way of learning. At other times it is the teacher who is the victim of self-inflicted incompetence and self-doubt and needing the therapeutic intervention of perpetual self-reflection on their own shortcomings.

I have seen it myself in teacher education where we have insisted that trainees engage in almost constant self-flagellation and where teaching sessions descend into therapeutic forms of facilitation so they become more like primary school circle time. Teaching becomes more like a counselling session than an examination, exploration and rigorous challenge of trainee teachers' knowledge. In one particular instance when I challenged a trainee's sociological knowledge, another student remonstrated with me because I had attacked her colleague. I pointed out that questioning the accuracy and efficacy of subject knowledge is not a personal attack, but an integral aspect of learning to become a teacher. Therapeutic professionalism and regulatory professionalism are not contradictory. Together they bestow on us a veneer of authority of a spurious kind. No longer in charge of our students' minds, we are reduced to being responsible for only their emotions and well-being, and we are held to account through endless bureaucratic processes, where our professionalism lies in responsibility for numerical rather than intellectual growth.

## Beyond professionalism

So can we reclaim professionalism? Maybe this is the wrong question to ask. In *The Rise of Professionalism: A Sociological Analysis*, Larson suggests that we need to replace the old notions of professionalism as they are obscuring our reality.

> The conditions of professional work have changed so that the predominant pattern is no longer that of the free practitioner in a market of services, but that of the salaried specialist in a large organization. In this age of corporate capitalism, the model of profession nevertheless retains its vigour; it is still something to be defended or something to be obtained by occupations in a different historical context, in radically different work settings, and in radically altered forms of practice. The persistence of profession as a category of social practice suggests that the model constituted by the first movements of professionalism has become an ideology – not only an image which consciously inspires collective or individual efforts, but a mystification which unconsciously obscures real social structures and relations.
>
> (Larson, 1979: xviii)

In other words, we cannot pretend that a model that applied 100 years ago still applies today. So the question is not can we reclaim our profession, but can we reconstruct it? My solution is that we need to go out of control. It is time to move from subversion to revolution. To rebuild anything that might be called professionalism, it is essential to throw out old notions and redefine with new ones. There is no point in asking permission or trying to reform existing bodies.

To refashion our professionalism there are three core elements we must reclaim.

We must reclaim our expertise in pedagogy. We are the keepers of the secret chalice of knowledge, not OFSTED, not politicians, and certainly not students. To use another metaphor, pedagogy is Samson's hair. In our pedagogical knowledge lies the authority and professional core of being a teacher. By giving it away, even if we think we're doing so in a subversive way, we give away all claims to our independence and professionalism. And that knowledge is not just theoretical. It is the knowledge at the core of life. Whatever our discipline, whether we are teaching calculus or car maintenance, we are the authority on our subject. We must be the font of all subject knowledge for our students.

We must reclaim our authority in the classroom and beyond by reclaiming our autonomy. Autonomy in this case is not an individual teacher's right to do as they please, but rather a professional autonomy, based on our pedagogical authority individually and collectively as a community of knowledge. Reclaiming the authority of the teacher can only happen when we reclaim the autonomy of the collective and that in turns supports the autonomy of the individual professional.

We must reclaim education as a discipline. Teachers are made, and we are made through a process that initiates us into the discipline that is education. We need to reclaim teacher education as the intellectual discipline that it should be. Not the insipid training to jump through competency and standards hoops, coupled with the exhortation to self-flagellate on a regular basis (the one called professional reflection), but the initiation into the philosophy, sociology, psychology and history of education that are the foundations on which our new professional temple is to be built.

The choice is ours and it is stark. We can become autonomous, authoritative professionals or we can continue to be led by the nose. We must break down the door and tell the king in no uncertain terms not just that we will dance but that we are the composers and the choreographers of the music and the dance.

And if we must use metaphors then allow me my own metaphor. It is not that of the hapless or even subversive princess. If FE is anything, it is the fairy godmother. The one who waves the magic wand and gives everyone a second chance: the 16 year old who left school disillusioned; the 20-something forging ahead in a new vocation; the mid-30s learner who needs to update their qualification; the person in their 40s changing careers. FE makes it all possible. It is FE that is the saviour of the nation, especially as half the nation's teenagers still leave secondary school without the prerequisite GCSEs to progress.

The twelve princesses may have been dancing secretly for years, with FE teachers publicly acquiescing to being locked within policy and managerial confines, while persisting in doing their own thing surreptitiously, but this clandestine dancing must come to an end. It is high time the princesses defy the king, own up to their subversive activity and out themselves as the great dancers they are. It is time we restore our autonomy and voice, rather than persisting in living this double life that is keeping us under the metaphorical lock and key, and eroding our professionalism. The king will never allow the princesses out to dance and we need to stop waiting for his permission. It's gone past the time of subversion. It's high time for revolution.

It is time to take over the castle!

# References

Arendt, H. (1961) *Between Past and Future: Six exercises in political thought*. New York: Viking Press.

Bell, D. (1970) *Royal Institute of Philosophy Lectures*, 4, 190–203.

Crook, D. (2008) 'Some historical perspectives on professionalism'. In Cunningham, B. (ed.) *Exploring Professionalism*. London: IOE.

Horton, M., and Freire, P. (1990) *We Make the Road by Walking: Conversations on education and social change*. Philadelphia: Temple University Press.

Larson, M. (1979) *The Rise of Professionalism: A sociological analysis*. Berkeley: University of California Press.

McCulloch, G. (2011) *The Struggle for the History of Education*. London: Routledge.

Morris, E. (2001) 'Professionalism and trust: The future of teachers and teaching'. Speech by the Secretary of State for Education and Skills to the Social Market Foundation. London: Department for Education and Skills.

Schön, D.A. (1983) *The Reflective Practitioner: How professionals think in action*. New York: Basic Books.

Young, M. (2012) 'The Curriculum – "An entitlement to powerful knowledge": A response to John White'. *New Visions for Education*. 3 May. Online. http://www.newvisionsforeducation.org.uk/2012/05/03/the-curriculum-'an-entitlement-to-powerful-knowledge'-a-response-to-john-white/ (accessed 1 April 2015).

# Conclusion: Leading a merry dance through times of change and challenge

*Yvonne Hillier*

> '*Dance is a moment, and then it is finished, I do not believe durability is one of the great virtues. I don't think I would appreciate a lily that has been embalmed. There will be other dancers.*'
>
> (José Limón)

Throughout this book we have been examining the policy and practice of FE through the metaphor of the twelve dancing princesses who managed to wrest some independence from their father. We have variously talked about submission versus subversion, deviousness versus outright insubordination and even suggested that dancing was fun in the process. We have drawn upon research undertaken over the past two decades into the experiences of staff from the sector to demonstrate that there is both strategic compliance (Bathmaker, 2006) but also principled infidelity (Wallace and Hoyle, 2007: 88). By now, you, the reader, will have gained a strong impression of the complexity and overwhelming state of flux that the sector experiences at national, regional and local levels. We have shown how the demand for a professional workforce has shaped initial teacher education and continuing professional development. We have examined the pervasive metaphor of Cinderella, with the middle child an alternative. It would be easy to conclude that folk who work in FE are downtrodden, disheartened and disempowered. Yet, as our dancing princesses show, it is possible to manage a given context towards a resolution that makes living, and in this case working, more than a compromise.

In this concluding chapter, I would like to draw upon four lenses that bring into sharper focus this complex and truly chaotic sector. These are the lenses of identity, agency, tension and deliberative spaces. They arise from research conducted ten years ago into the policy and practice of adult literacy, language and numeracy (ALLN), which interviewed nearly 200 practitioners, managers and policy makers in the field (Hamilton and Hillier, 2006; Hillier, 2009). I show how one network over the past 18 years has managed to develop and support the professional practice of teachers in the sector, i.e. to lead a merry dance through times of change and challenge.

## Identity

If we look at the identity of professionals in the sector, we can see in Taubman's chapter that being professional has many definitions and consequences. The governmental approach to professionalism has waxed and waned in relation to expectations of knowledge of teaching and learning demonstrated through qualifications, but there is an underlying expectation that there is a body of knowledge and expertise that can be audited to ensure that students in the system meet set standards and expectations. This approach is at variance with Taubman's view, in Chapter 8, that professionalism should be underpinned by a set of values and that these include social justice, equality, democracy, sustainability, well-being and creativity. There is nothing wrong with checking how well teachers enable their students to learn, and having a set of expectations of the ways in which they do so. The difficulty is that it is hard to establish an overarching, agreed standard that is flexible enough to account for the many contexts in which FE teachers practise and serves to enhance their work in a developmental and democratic way.

Being professional, then, is subject to many interpretations and influences. Given the position of FE in relation to HE or indeed schools, people who work in the sector are battling against wider issues, including the status of their work.

> Given the basic importance of vocational learning for economic success, it is remarkable that its practitioners so lack the level of social recognition needed to establish it as a well-regarded profession that attracts societal affirmation as well as attracting appropriate individuals to practise as vocational educators.
>
> (Misra, 2011: 31)

If we turn to international comparisons, we find that in many European countries there is a distinction in nomenclature between teachers and practitioners. For example, in Germany, Denmark and to a certain extent the UK, teachers work in educational institutions, vocational education and training (VET) practitioners work in enterprises and organizations, whereas in Belgium and France teachers work in initial vocational education but practitioners undertake continuing VET. In other parts of Europe, teachers do theory and VET practitioners do practice (Greece and Spain). We also have distinctions between the craftsman-turned-teacher tradition, the general subject teacher tradition and the professional VET teacher (Belgium, Netherlands, Norway and Sweden). Generally, teachers of practical subjects are seen to need less pre-service education than those teaching theoretical or general subjects. Yet the highly fluid changes in the learning environment and in society more generally mean that VET teachers and trainers are under constant pressure to update their professional knowledge and practice. Anyone working in FE today might well be expected not only to teach but also mentor, guide and counsel students from a wide range of cultural backgrounds, undertake administrative work, design and manage curricula in their own subjects, as well as liaise with those of colleagues, and respond to frequent policy initiatives (Misra, 2011).

It would help to ask ourselves what kinds of professionals we want to be, in light of the work that we do. This is where the more dynamic, democratic concept of professionalism comes to the fore. Here, we argue that our identity as a professional is one of being autonomous, where we can be trusted to make decisions that are in the best interests of our students and our colleagues and where we take action to work towards the goals and values outlined above. Being active involves not just taking responsibility for decisions in our daily practice but thinking about what we do reflectively and actually trying out our ideas. It means experimenting, not just on our own in teaching environments that hardly anyone visits unless they are undertaking quality assurance or inspection. It means being with others. The twelve dancing princesses danced together. They belonged together as siblings. There is a strong identity among practitioners and teachers in their subject areas, their programme groups and to a lesser extent their institutions. These communities extend beyond the physical spaces (of which more later) but have strong bonds, with huge potential for taking action for developing professional practice together. Yet, as has been argued elsewhere in this book, many people in the sector do not necessarily realize they have this potential. And this brings me to my next lens, agency.

## Agency

As Hafez said in Chapter 12, it is high-time the dancing princesses stopped their subversion game, or waiting for permission from the king to dance. What do we mean by agency? Is it something that we possess in certain quantities? Do we have it at times and not at others? Can we instruct someone else to use their agency? In this story, the twelve dancing princesses were using their agency because they refused to simply abide by the king's rules and they took action to maximize their own wishes. In the FE sector, where people have many roles and responsibilities, they can act as change agents in subtle as well as overt ways. In our study of ALLN, Mary Hamilton and I found examples of teachers campaigning in national, high-profile ways (cuts to provision, protests against changes to pay and conditions, giving evidence to parliament) as well as work within local governing bodies, committees and programme teams. Today we can see this in current disputes about pay and conditions in some institutions and, as shown in Chapter 11, the successful campaign in ESOL. In all these examples, what is happening is that people are trying to do the best they can, without necessarily knowing what will help deal with complex but concrete issues.

> We see practitioners of very different plumage wrestle with conflict, power, uncertainty and unpredictability. Solutions are not so much formulated as arrived at, haltingly, tentatively, through acting upon the situation at hand and through the application of practical wisdom in negotiating concrete situations.
>
> (Hajer and Wagenaar, 2003: 18)

It is because the contexts are so contested that the next lens, tension, is so useful for examining FE.

## Tension

As Rouxel argued in Chapter 10, there is tension in the system where judgements are being made for improvement, which at first sight seem out of the hands of those who are actually doing the work that determines the criteria by which they are being judged. Tension is inherent within any system and FE is no exception. Throughout this book, we have shown how practitioners have to manage competing demands, find ways to uphold their own values in responding to the performativity and managerialist nature of the current regime, as well as make sense of their own subject expertise in often fast-changing contexts where knowledge appears ever more tentative and precarious. Many tensions in the system are enduring and have to be managed; they are not problems to be solved. The deeply held value of putting students at the forefront of our work does not mean that we all agree on the best way to achieve this. Indeed, in any programme team there will be debates about changes to curricula and teaching environments. There will be champions and dissenters. We have only to consider the path that led to learning technology becoming part of the backdrop in any classroom to see how teachers did not always share the vision of educational technology. Even today, there are those who simply refuse to embrace it and those who do so completely.

Tension is unsettling. It can act as a spur to action. A consequence of tension in the system is that many people use their agency to resist, by varying means, whatever they find unacceptable, and the book contains many examples of this. The reverse can occur where deciding not to act becomes a means to manage the tension experienced. We can see tension in our system at all levels: between government demands for a more economically successful workforce, educated through FE versus a more liberal or radical approach to learning (see for example: Coffield, 2008; Brookfield, 1995); between linear academic qualifications and course-based, continually assessed work; between generic literacy and numeracy teaching and embedded, linked skills within subject disciplines. We can see tension between managers and teachers, between FE and HE systems, between schools and FE.

Yet my final lens, deliberative spaces, shows where there is opportunity for people in the sector to use their agency, to manage the tensions that influence their practice and to undertake this practice in ways that align with their professional identity.

## Deliberative spaces

> Participants in policy making all do so from different positions in space-time, with different experiences, stakes, values, norms and beliefs. The possibility of creative action may become a reality only if they manage to create some common or shared understandings on why they seek cooperation and collective action at all. The essential process therefore is the joint construction of problems as a condition for joint responses.
>
> (Hoppe, 2010: 50)

Where are the spaces for deliberate, reflexive action? Where can practitioners go beyond survival, to re-energize, to reclaim their identities and act in ways that give them freedom to 'be themselves'? Where, in other words, as Weatherby and Mycroft ask in Chapter 5 (68), is the space to 'go off and dance where and how we want, dance, with freedom to be present as ourselves?' Space is mentioned throughout this book: space for intervention, space to cross boundaries, space to dance, space to work out what to do. Space is conceived as physical space, emotional space, thinking space, space for changing practice, changing identity, space for protest. A deliberative space occurs where there are opportunities and what would now be called affordances.

In our sector, such spaces have become established, grown and withered, to be replaced by others. For example, in the early 1980s, awarding bodies provided space for then moderators and assessors, as they were called, to meet together to share good practice from visits they had made to the colleges in their own specialist subject area. This was a deliberative space, supported by awarding bodies, which could influence the professional practice in the field. When the national vocational qualification system was introduced and competence-based qualifications ensued, the practice of moderation and assessment was replaced by verification and the deliberative space for sharing good practice, provided by awarding bodies, gradually ceased as demands for a different form of quality assurance took place. Yet other forms of deliberative space grew, such as particular initiatives including the Centres of Vocational Excellence (COVEs) which were supported by the then Learning and Skills Development Agency (LSDA). In both examples, practitioners were able to meet together physically, share practice and ideas and have time away from their institutions for thinking and developing with colleagues.

Not all spaces need to be organized by formal institutions. The growth of social networks has enabled practitioner-led space to develop and now such spaces do not require physical space or even people to be meeting together synchronously. As Appleby and Hillier (2012) found, networks of practitioners that are developed outside formal spaces provide different opportunities to discuss and debate issues that arise from the implementation of top-down initiatives. In other words, deliberative spaces do provide the context for agency and where necessary, to act in ways that minimize the worst excesses of policies and programmes that undermine the values that are held by practitioners in the field.

## A particular dance: The Learning and Skills Research Network (LSRN)

Years ago, most people in FE did not consider themselves researchers as part of their everyday role and most research that was conducted about the sector was done by academic researchers from HE. Yet people *were* experimenting, trying out new ideas, individually or collaboratively, as they introduced new programmes and new ways of learning, particularly with the early beginnings of computer use. One of the agencies responsible for supporting the work of FE, the then Further Education Development Agency (FEDA), ran a three-day workshop on research in the sector and this culminated in a decision to set up a research network for people in FE, to undertake research in the sector and to disseminate it to their colleagues. In January 1997 a first national planning meeting took place and thus was spawned what became the Learning and Skills Research Network (LSRN). Its story has been told more fully elsewhere (Hillier and Morris, 2010) but there are characteristics of this network that bear scrutiny, in relation to our twelve dancing princesses.

When it was created, it was clear that LSRN needed a set of values and principles. It was also obvious that there was little formalized research in the field by those who worked in the field and there was no deliberative space for people to meet together and share their research. An early decision was taken to launch a journal aimed specifically at staff in the sector, which would be accessible but also reputable, alongside the establishment of what was to become an annual research conference. Here academics and policy makers were welcomed but the primary aim was to encourage delegates from the FE sector to have a place and space to hear about academic research of their sector, and to be encouraged to undertake research themselves.

At the first conference, delegates were given a chance to meet in regional groups and each group decided to form a regional network, convened by a volunteer but supported by regional managers from FEDA (which later became the Learning and Skills Development Agency, LSDA). Such networks established regional conferences, regular meetings and opportunities to make use of the emerging research that was beginning to be disseminated through the research journal and through other more formal development initiatives.

The conferences were so successful that awards were given to the best papers from those in the sector and these eventually formed the basis of an edited book (Hillier and Thompson, 2005). At the same time, LSDA provided funds to support regional projects and these, too, were collaborations by members from FE and HE, as well as adult education and work-based learning, parts of what was now called the lifelong learning sector. The projects led to further development, publication of reports and for many who participated in the projects, further research and developments. Eventually, the model of practitioner research was taken up by the National Research and Development Centre for Adult Literacy, Numeracy and Language (NRDC) and on to the Research Fellowships of the then Learning and Skills Improvement Service (LSIS) and more recently the Education and Training Foundation (ETF).

Yet there were tensions. Some established researchers in HE were sceptical of the appropriateness of an FE-based research network encouraging practitioners to undertake research without full and systematic training in research methods. Managers might support certain kinds of research that would lead to meeting performance targets (how best to recruit and retain learners for funding purposes!). The debates around the status of qualitative versus quantitative approaches to research and the quality of small-scale research versus large-scale data gathering ensued. Those most involved were giving time to the activity in ways that not all their institutions would have been happy with. Resources for meetings or time spent on activities might all be legitimate to some extent, but often people were volunteering and donating gift time, particularly those drawn from the FE sector, where research was definitely not seen to be a legitimate part of their role.

This story, though, is of a deliberative space that has continued to exist because the players, without realizing it, were subverting the system individually and collectively. They were challenging the idea that people in FE could not be equal partners in research or indeed lead research. They challenged the idea that people would not want to be involved in research and they certainly challenged managers in the system to support research in their own institutions. A lucky happenstance of not aligning themselves to one organization meant that when LSDA was disbanded, LSRN could continue. It did so by inviting key players from the system (awarding bodies, agencies, HE research centres) to a seminar to ask whether there was any interest in continuing the work of LSRN, now that a space had been created through the changing fortunes of LSDA. As a result, LSRN continues its work, supported by key players. Yet LSRN has no funding, no articles of association, no physical space. It exists and continues to exist, because of the activity of its members. Its situation is precarious but active and ever responsive to the changing context in which it exists.

## Still dancing...
Who knows what awaits us as we move forward into the coming years? We can't fix all the problems of our sector. We can't remove the tensions that are inherent, although we can do our best to minimize the impact of damaging policy decisions on our students and on our colleagues. If we really want to change the way our sector is viewed, we do have to confront those issues of status and power. We work among some of the most highly creative and talented folk in education. Teachers and practitioners have taught across ages and stages, across all levels and they have worked in some of the most demanding and difficult contexts. It is time for us to lead the merry dance and show just what fun we can have when we do.

## References
Appleby, Y., and Hillier, Y. (2012) 'Exploring practice-research networks for critical professional learning'. *Studies in Continuing Education*, 34 (1), 31–43.

Bathmaker, A.-M. (2006) 'Alternative Futures: Professional identity formation in English FE'. In Salterthwaite, J., Marting, W., and Roberts, L. (eds) *Discourse, Resistance and Identity Formation*. Stoke-on-Trent: Trentham.

Brookfield, S. (1995) *Becoming a Critically Reflective Teacher*. San Francisco: Jossey-Bass.

Coffield, F. (2008) *Running Ever Faster Down the Wrong Road: An alternative future for education and skills*. Inaugural Professorial Lecture, Institute of Education, University of London.

Hajer, M., and Wagenaar, H. (2003) (eds) *Deliberative Policy Analysis: Understanding governance in the network society*. Cambridge: Cambridge University Press.

Hamilton, M., and Hillier, Y. (2006) *Changing Faces of Adult Literacy, Language and Numeracy: A critical history*. Stoke-on-Trent: Trentham Books.

Hillier, Y. (2009) 'The changing faces of adult literacy, language and numeracy: literacy policy and implementation in the UK'. *Compare: A journal of comparative education*, 39 (4), 531–46.

Hillier, Y., and Morris, A. (2010) 'Critical practitioners, developing researchers: The story of practitioner research in the learning and skills sector'. *Journal of Vocational Education and Training*, 61 (1), 85–97.

Hillier, Y., and Thompson, A. (eds) (2005) *Readings in Post-Compulsory Research*. London: Continuum.

Hoppe, R. (2010) *The Governance of Problems: Puzzling, powering, participation*. Bristol: Policy Press.

Misra, P.K. (2011) 'VET teachers in Europe: Policies, practices and challenges'. *Journal of Vocational Education and Training*, 63 (1), 27–45.

Wallace, M., and Hoyle, E. (2007) 'An ironic perspective on public service change'. In Wallace, M., Fertig, M., and Schneller, E. (eds) *Managing Change in the Public Services*. Oxford: Blackwell.

# Coda: Writing as resistance
## *Kevin Orr*

*'Let's dance.'*
            (David Bowie)

The enthusiasm of all the contributors characterized the writing of this book. All have relished the opportunity to highlight aspects of FE about which they feel passionate. As Lou Mycroft puts it, 'this is a book for educators who haven't got cynical', or at least not about what matters in education: students, teachers and learning. We have enjoyed summoning our twelve dancing princesses as an antidote to the dreary metaphor of FE as Cinderella waiting for her dreary prince. But the playfulness of the dancing metaphor is deceptive because this book is also about resistance. FE is threatened by the introduction of competition in place of local planning; it is threatened by measures of quality that ignore what is meaningful when what is meaningful is difficult to measure; and it is threatened by encroaching privatization of the hitherto public provision of education.

These are the consequences of policy based on the ideology that free markets are the most efficient means to develop all aspects of society. Where markets do not exist, such as in education, the state must create them; or as Margaret Thatcher used to say, There Is No Alternative to individual entrepreneurial freedom and the pursuit of profit. Even allies referred to her as TINA. This ideology is neoliberalism, which has been identified in these chapters as the pernicious justification for decisions ranging from designing colleges to look like shopping malls, to the withdrawal of funding for ESOL classes. David Harvey (2005: 3) argues that neoliberalism 'has pervasive effects on ways of thought, to the point where it has been incorporated into the common-sense way many of us interpret, live in, and understand the world'. It has certainly pervaded the management of FE and rendered students as units of income or as one of Rebecca Maxted's participants puts it 'bearers of grades'.

This does not, however, have to be so. There is nothing natural about the organization of education based on market competition. Of course, education can make money but, to paraphrase Frank Coffield, that is not what education is for. Another FE is possible. So how do we challenge these policies? How do we challenge the spurious common sense of economic austerity that is destroying our colleges? Many of the contributors to this collection are trade-union activists and unions have a major role in this challenge, as demonstrated by the University and College Union's Manifesto for Post-School Education. Importantly, though, the successful campaigns described in this book, against compulsory fees for membership of the IfL or in support of ESOL provision, found their impetus from a coalition of ordinary teachers. These campaigns were collective – they had to be to have a chance of winning – but they were initiated by individuals who dared to defy and then to organize. These campaigns subsequently emboldened others who had felt marginal or powerless, rarely more so than in the case of ESOL students.

Writing can also be a form of resistance, and writing this book has in its own way involved a broad coalition to challenge dominant, damaging ideas about education. Our hope is that it may also embolden others to defy and then encourage them to organize and to dance.

## Reference

Harvey, D. (2005) *A Brief History of Neoliberalism.* New York: Oxford University Press.

# Index